PERGAMON INSTITUTE OF ENGLISH (OXFORD)

Language Teaching Methodology Series

COUNSELING AND CULTURE

N

SECOND LANGUAGE ACQUISITION

Other titles in this series

COUNSELING AND CULTURE
IN
SECOND LANGUAGE ACQUISITION

PAUL G. LA FORGE
Nanzan Junior College,
Nagoya, Japan

Pergamon Press
Oxford · New York · Toronto · Sydney · Paris · Frankfurt

U.K.	Pergamon Press Ltd., Headington Hill Hall, Oxford OX3 0BW, England
U.S.A.	Pergamon Press Inc., Maxwell House, Fairview Park, Elmsford, New York 10523, U.S.A.
CANADA	Pergamon Press Canada Ltd., Suite 104, 150 Consumers Road, Willowdale, Ontario M2J 1P9, Canada
AUSTRALIA	Pergamon Press (Aust.) Pty. Ltd., P.O. Box 544, Potts Point, N.S.W. 2011, Australia
FRANCE	Pergamon Press SARL, 24 rue des Ecoles, 75240 Paris, Cedex 05, France
FEDERAL REPUBLIC OF GERMANY	Pergamon Press GmbH, Hammerweg 6, D-6242 Kronberg-Taunus, Federal Republic of Germany

First edition 1983

Library of Congress Cataloging in Publication Data

La Forge, Paul G.
Counseling and culture in second language acquisition.
(Materials for language practice) (Language teaching methodology series)
Bibliography: p.
Includes index.
1. Language and languages—Study and teaching.
2. Counseling.   3. Educational anthropology.
I. Title.   II. Series.   III. Series: Language teaching methodology series.
P53.L28   1983   418'.007   82-22581

British Library Cataloguing in Publication Data

La Forge, Paul G.
Counseling and culture in second language acquisition.
1. Language and languages—Study and teaching
2. Language acquisition
I. Title
401'.9   P53
ISBN 0-08-029477-4

Contents

Introduction

0.1. Second Language Acquisition

This book is about second language acquisition. In general, second language acquisition refers to the teaching and learning of foreign and/or other second language. The application of counseling to this field was pioneered by Charles A. Curran. Since his premature passing, new developments have occurred in counseling, linguistics, and experimental psychology. These developments warrant a fresh approach to the problem of foreign language learning. The foreign language teacher has been a rather passive receiver of information from other fields in the past. This volume attempts, upon digestion and trial of new insights from other fields, to propose avenues of research which linguists, psychologists, and even anthropologists might pursue. At the same time, the examples and conclusions derived from the classroom will be of primary benefit to foreign language teachers. The main thrust of this work is to present examples of learning which stay beyond the narrow confines of a single teaching-learning methodology. The Japanese case with Counseling Learning/Community Language Learning merely clarifies the issues and presents classroom activities which teachers elsewhere can easily adopt, accommodate or reject. The clarification of issues, it is hoped, will assist teachers to a better understanding of the difficult task of acquiring a foreign language. More effective learning will be the ultimate result.

0.2. Counseling

A distinction must be made between therapeutic, integrative, and task-oriented counseling. Therapeutic counseling benefits those with problems in basic human functioning. Integrative counseling helps those who wish to review and improve their interpersonal relationships. T-Group training is a good example of integrative counseling. The communicative focus for both these types of counseling is upon affective factors in learning. The attempt in therapeutic counseling is to solve affective problems. In integrative counseling, the focus is centered on gaining insights into interpersonal relationships through dwelling on the affects. By way of contrast, the focus of task-oriented counseling is on cognitive communication. Affective factors are important, but play an essentially subordinate role. These distinctions may assist teachers to be more comfortable with a Counseling-Learning approach to second language acquisition.

Among the multitude of factors which one meets in the classroom, three have struck me as most basic: first, language learning is people; second, language learning is persons in dynamic interaction; third, language learning is persons in response. Language learning is people: this is the basic social process of learning. Learning, the acquisition of second language, occurs in an interpersonal relationship between a teacher and a group of students, as well as among the students themselves. Dynamic interaction means that persons are given birth and grow in foreign language. Their relationships change as they develop in the language. Dynamic interaction means that the teacher provides meaningful learning experiences which fit the needs of the learners at various stages of their development.

0.3. Culture

Language learning is also response by the learners. Anyone who deals with Japanese learners, for example, is quickly made aware of a long tradition of learning to which they are very attached. Even Japanese members of a community language learning group do not hesitate to assert their preferences and demands in a strong and forceful manner. Given a social process based on Counseling-Learning and Community Language Learning, Japanese students react and form a creative learning relationship with their teacher according to the norms of their culture. This presents a dilemma for the teacher. On the one hand, he can react in fear that the learning goal may become clouded or lost by the emphasis on culture. On the other hand, however, he may adopt the culture norm. The use of culture norms together with a viable pedagogy enhances learning, as will be shown in the Japanese case with community language learning. Social and cultural processes mutually strengthen each other and cannot be totally separated. Both operate to form a supportive learning milieu in which the individual grows. The clarification of social process and the unfolding of the creative response, culture, form two overlapping themes of this book. An overview is presented in Chapter 1.

0.4. Acknowledgements

The author is particularly indebted to the Society of the Divine Word for continued support over the years. The English faculty of Nanzan Junior College, Nagoya, have provided useful suggestions and support. Mr. P. Lance Knowles and the faculty of the Language Institute of Japan at Odawara deserve a rich measure of credit for their support of the preliminary research. Mr. William Gatton provided literary assistance in preparing the manuscript for publication. Even the students of Saint John's Hostel, Nagoya, come in for a final word. They agreed to read and criticize the manuscript at crucial points during its composition. Proof reading the manuscript, always a laborious task, was undertaken by Raymond Donahue, Sherraid Scott, James Landkammer, David Kluge, Patrick and Donna Buckheister. To these, and especially to the students of Nanzan Junior College, the author remains perpetually indebted.

January 1983   PAUL G. LA FORGE

The author wishes to gratefully acknowledge the release of previously published materials:

Material in Chapters 3, 4, 5, 6 and 9 first appeared in *Cross Currents, a Journal of Communication, Language, Cross Cultural Skills.*

Material used in Chapter 10 was first published in *Humanistic Approaches: An Empirical View*, ELT Documents 113, 1982 and is reproduced here with the kind permission of the British Council.

A fuller version of Chapter 7 first appeared in *ELT Journal*, (Vol XXXIII/4, 247–54), published by Oxford University Press and the British Council.

Material on social silence (Chapter 6) first appeared in the *TESOL Quarterly*, 1979, Vol. 11, 373–82. This was the last issue edited by the late Ruth Crymes, to whom the author remains indebted for her patient assistance during the preparation of the manuscript.

Material in Chapters 3 and 9 first appeared in a different form in *Language in Japanese Society: Current Issues in Sociolinguistics*. Fred C. C. Peng (Ed.), Tokyo: University of Tokyo Press, 1975.

Material on cultural silence (Chapter 6) first appeared in *IRLT News Letter*, Tokyo.

Chapter 9 first appeared in *Topics in Culture Learning*, 1976, Vol. 4, East–West Center, Honolulu. The author remains grateful for the encouragement of Dr. Richard Brislin, Larry Smith, Richard Via and others of the East–West Culture Learning Institute.

0.5. Dedication

To twenty-five years in the Roman Catholic Priesthood.

Chapter 1
A Social Process Model of Language for Language Teaching - Learning

1.0. Language as Social Process

Perhaps the most significant feature of twentieth-century intellectual development has been the way in which language has been reinterpreted as social process. A process view of language has opened the route to an understanding of mankind, social history, and the laws of how a society functions. All social practices can be seen as languages (Coward and Ellis, 1977, 1). This development is based on several assumptions. First, all social practices can be understood as contracts, that is, the negotiation of reciprocal meanings, agreements on mutual expectations, the discovery of interpersonal signification and two-way circuits of exchange between subjects. The subjects involved are people who exchange experiences. Out of the experiences may come guides to behavior. These guides give direction to life and may be called "values." Values are subject to contract negotiation, and control what is done with space, time, and energy. Second, because all the practices that make up a social totality take place in language, it becomes possible to consider language as the place in which the social individual is constructed. A process view of language has created the study of man as "subject," that is, the individual in society as a language-using social and historical entity. Third, the intersection of the social, historical, individual, and cultural, underlies the concept of man as language. Man is not only a producer, but is also in creative and dynamic response. His personal development and culture take place in language through group response. A social process view of language means that language is people, persons in contact, and persons in response.

The process view of language contains important implications for language teaching–learning. The purpose of this chapter is to introduce such a model to theoretical linguists and foreign language teachers. There are six qualities which can be derived from a process view of language. The six qualities will be introduced briefly, then exemplified more fully in later chapters of this book. First, since language is people in contract, the *whole-person process* must be considered both in cognition and affect. Whole-person process can be shown at the moment of understanding in counseling psychology (Curran, 1969, 43). Whole-person process begins with the person of the scientist, as will be shown in Chapter 2. Second, teaching–learning may be differentiated from other forms of social process, such as group psychotherapy and T-Group counseling, by the focus upon the cognitive task, ie, the *educational process*. Third, since language is people, the goal must be a mutual one which is acquired in the *interpersonal process* of a group or community. Educational process includes interpersonal or social dimensions of learning and will be considered in Chapter 3. Fourth, since the social individual is constructed and developed in language, a model for teaching–learning must account for the *developmental processes* of those involved. Developmental processes will be taken up in Chapters 4 and 5. Whole-person process includes psychosomatic communication of a non-verbal order termed *communicative process*. Communicative process will be treated later as silence and reflection in Chapters 6 and 7. Since language is response, the response of the learners must also be taken into account. Group response can be considered as *cultural process* and forms a second theme of this book.

PART 1: TO THEORETICAL LINGUISTS

1.1. The Process Model

The process model for language and language teaching can be derived from a counseling model developed by the late Charles A. Curran of Loyola University of Chicago (1968, 295–322; 1969, 43, 211–27; 1972; 1976; 1978a; 1978b) and is presented here in contrast to current teaching–learning models from theoretical linguistics. First, the social process model is different from one of language as communication. Second, models from theoretical linguistics have systematically eliminated essentials of the social process, namely, person, contract and response. Third, considerations of social constraints and interpersonal interaction, as is shown in sociolinguistics, cannot be ignored if we are to develop an adequate theory of language. As social practice, language teaching–learning should lean on linguistics as a model for the elaboration of its systematic reality. Because of the elimination of social process in linguistics, language teachers have had to look elsewhere for viable teaching–learning models. Theoretical linguists have relegated important and promising areas of fruitful research in language and language teaching–learning to the perimeters of their field. Examples include sociolinguistics, paralinguistics and semiology. Just those areas which are considered peripheral by theoretical linguists are becoming of great importance to the teacher of foreign language.

1.1.1. Language as Communication

A social process view of language is different from the concept of language as communication. The fundamental problem with the latter concept, according to Coward and Ellis (1977, 79), is that it tends to obscure the way in which language sets up the positions of "I" and "You" that are necessary for communication to take place at all. Communication is more than just a message being transmitted from a speaker to a listener. The speaker is, at the same time, both the subject and object of his own message. He deciphers the message while speaking because he cannot say anything that he does not in some way understand. Thus the message which is intended for the other person is in one sense also intended for the person who speaks. You talk to yourself from the place of the other. Communication involves not just the unidirectional transfer of information to the other, but the very constitution of the speaking subject in relation to its other. The speaker is not the sole possession of linguistics but also concerns psychoanalysis (Coward and Ellis, 1977, 80) and counseling psychology (Curran, 1972, 115). In both therapies the raw material is language. Communication is an exchange which is incomplete without a feedback reaction from the destinee of the message.

1.1.2. The Elimination of Social Process

How have person, contract, and response been systematically eliminated from consideration by modern linguistics? This can be seen in the methodology of some linguists, the criteria for linguistic data and the models which are proposed for language and language teaching–learning. According to Corder (1973, 159), method in linguistics has been called "idealization of data," which means the systematic process of selecting the relevant features (ie, those which remain constant in any context), and ignoring the irrelevant ones. Regularization of the data is the process of eliminating adventitious features such as slips of the tongue, hesitations, repetitions, changes of plan and so on (Corder, 1973, 159). Anything which is not part of language as system is eliminated. Language becomes a mere cognitive phenomenon from which all expression of overt and covert affects is removed. However, the study of just these irregularities and errors in the system, as a matter of history, led to the discovery of the covert expression of affects in the malfunctioning person. Attention to slips of the tongue, pauses, and silences in the speech of his patients in the social situation led Freud to uncover subconscious emotional blocks. These discoveries led to a new and dynamic concept of the person, a concept eliminated from linguistics through the regularization of data. Second, the process of standardization involves the elimination of all variability derived from the social and cultural characteristics of the producers of the data. By standardization, language is divorced from contract − personal, social, and cultural exchanges. Third, decontextualization is the removal of features of language use. The hearer has to supply some information from his understanding of the social order to be able to interpret the utterance of another. Decontextualization consists of "putting back" into the data those linguistic elements which have been "deleted" because they are "understood" from the context (Corder, 1973, 161). Response is distorted by decontextualization. For example, "Anyone seen Bill?" "In the garage." This would presumably be decontextualized as follows: "Has anyone seen Bill?" "Look in the garage." The linguistic method outlined here removes affect, person, social, and cultural process from language. The remainder forms a lifeless hulk called "Neutral Language" which "remains inadequate for any purpose" (Corder, 1973, 209).

1.1.3. Criteria for Language Theory

There are three criteria or "tools for the construction of language theory" (Peng, 1975, 14): sound features, the sentence, and abstract models of language. The sound features which are selected for linguistic description have their physical basis in their articulatory and acoustic characteristics. Sound is treated as a mere physical entity measurable in the dimensions of frequency, amplitude, and duration. According to Stevick (1976a, 277), linguists have told us that the phonetic details of pronunciation are the most superficial part of language. But beyond signaling changes of meaning, the symbolic value of subphonemic variants runs deeper into the personality, into the self-image of the learner, than semantics, syntax or phonological constructs. Since they have a connection with a picture of the self as a member of certain groups and a non-member of certain others, the usage of subphonemic variants gives rise to feelings of alienation or affiliation influencing the mastery of pronunciation (Stevick, 1976a, 227). The connection between sound features and deeper levels of the personality is usually discounted by linguists who regard sound as just another aspect of language.

The second criterion is the establishment of relevant descriptive units in phonology (phoneme, syllable), and in syntax (word, sentence). The meaning of all these terms has long been in dispute among linguists. Peng (1975, 13 & 14) has shown that the sentence is not the ultimate unit with which linguistics is concerned. The social environment, people and language itself, all three of which are lacking in the abstract formulations of some linguists, are necessary for an adequate understanding of language.

The third criterion is the construction of an adequate model for a description of language. Corder (1973, 179—97) has described three such models: linear, phrase structure, and transformational models. Linear and phrase structure models still influence the practice of language teaching—learning through the oral drill techniques of the language learning laboratory. But besides ignoring motivation, the constant repetition of sentences is not language learning. Corder emphasizes a description of the transformational model as a possible theoretical basis for language teaching. But at the end of his description he is forced to admit:

Do we have available any linguistic description of language performance? The answer is: No, none of the linguistic descriptions yet provides a systematic account of performance. We must judge that linguistic descriptions fall short, by definition, of what is needed by the applied linguist (1973, 197).

1.1.4. The Transformational Model

The transformational model proposed for second language acquisition is devoid of personal and social functions required for communication in any language. As presented by Richards (1976, 118), it consists of an abstract model of six levels. The first two consist of code storage and particular arrangements activated to represent a given meaning. These two levels are conceptual and cognitive in nature and are independent of language. Supposedly, these levels contain a description of the ideal speaker—hearer's intrinsic competence. The other four levels refer to performance and are linguistic and language-dependent. Level 3 consists of the ability to match and select the linguistic categories required for syntactic and lexical expression. Level 4 contains the rules for deep and surface syntax relations and morphology. Levels 5 and 6 are the rules necessary for correct phonology and articulation. None of these terms are very clearly explained with reference to learners in our classes. Certainly, our students do not fit the model of the ideal speaker—hearer existing in a completely homogeneous speech community. The ideal being who knows his language perfectly, simply does not exist. Common sense demands recognition of the fact that everyone is affected by such grammatically-irrelevant conditions as memory limitations, distractions, shifts of attention and interest, and errors (random or characteristic). In all justice, the model was not proposed for second language acquisition by Chomsky himself. Others have proposed it more clearly, and, in some cases, less clearly (Richards, 1976, 118; Saporta, 1966/1973; Corder, 1973).

1.1.5. Social Constraints

An interesting description of language by Crystal and Davy (1969, 1973) has been proposed not by abstracting from, but by starting with social process and its constraints. Most of the segmental phonology of English, and most of the grammatical and lexical patterns are imposed on the language user as laws common to the whole community in all situations. The entire range of linguistic features in a social context is plotted. The notion of situation is broken down into "dimensions of situation constraint," which are referred to rather loosely as "situational variables" (Crystal and Davy, 1969/1973, 73). The role every feature plays is described in terms of one or more of these dimensions. Of the eight dimensions listed, three are stylistically neutral or "common core" features which occur regardless of the other situational dimensions. Discourse, province, status, modality and singularity are usually restricted in some way by the social situation. Space does not allow a more detailed description of grammatical categories. The point is that once the situational dimensions have been set up, the phonological, grammatical, and lexical description follows and can even be predicted. Crystal and Davy have written as follows:

> One should also note the corollary, that with the description of dimensions so far described, there is a powerful mutual predictability between language and situation: if the relevant extra-linguistic factors are known, then certain linguistic features will be readily predictable and vice-versa (1969/1973, 76).

1.1.6. Language as Interpersonal Development

Considered in the perspective of language development as a whole, the latest period of intensive study in the field, within the past decade or more, has been characterized by a rather one-sided concentration on grammatical structure. The implication, according to Halliday (1975, 1), has been that the acquisition of structure is really the heart of the learning process. The dominant standpoint has been a psycholinguistic one with its stress on the development of the cognitive structure of language. As a sociolinguistic process, language has been reinterpreted by Halliday as interaction between the child and other human beings. From this perspective, the focus of attention is on the linguistic system as a whole with meaning potential (semantic system) at one end and a vocal potential (phonological system) at the other. Grammatical structure no longer occupies the center of the stage; it enters in because it is one form of realization of meanings. The concept of language as social process has important consequences for theoretical linguistics which must be worked out by linguists themselves. Theoretical linguistics will not lose its identity as an independent science through contacts with other fields such as psychology, sociology, and language teaching—learning. Much to the contrary, an enriched concept of language will be the result of our mutual efforts to understand the theory and function of language from many viewpoints. I would now like to turn to the process model for language teaching—learning, describe its six qualities and show how scattered areas of linguistic research may be integrated around a process model for language.

PART 2: TO FOREIGN LANGUAGE TEACHERS

1.2. Psychological Counseling

A process model for language teaching—learning was developed by Curran, who noted two steps in counseling which are vital to the concept of language as social process (1969, 43). In step one, understanding begins with the client presenting his problem to the counselor. In a confused way, the client senses problems that prevent effective and creative functioning in his daily activities. These are "affective binds." The client's depression, anxiety, or anger, are a source of conflict and suffering for himself and those around him. When the client enters counseling, he begins to voice his affects in language. This is called "release in affective language."

The language of the client is heard by the counselor who exercises "creative listening." More is involved in creative listening than receiving linguistic signals from the client. The counselor not only hears the client's message, he also receives visual cues from the client's psychosomatic attitude. The counselor responds to what he hears, sees, and feels is the client's message. He then translates the communication of affects from the client into his own cognitive understanding of the problem.

Step two is the, response of the counselor in "cognitive language." The counselor is not involved in the same affects as the client. According to Curran (1969, 44), emotional involvement in the same affects would constitute a blind spot which would impede the counselor's awareness of what the client is trying to communicate. As the counselor listens, he tries to symbolize in a cognitive way what the client is actually feeling. The counselor puts this in language conveying the meaning disentangled from its confused affect. In response, the client evaluates the appropriateness of the counselor's translation. If the cognition language of the counselor does not fit the affect of the client, the response will be negative: "No, that is not what I mean!" As a result of the counselor's inaccuracy, the client remains bound up in his affects. If the counselor's reply accurately reflects the affects of the client, the effect is an immediate feeling of relief: "Yes, that's it!" The release of the affect which has kept the client bound, now gives him the freedom to delve deeper and deeper into himself and his situation as the process is repeated. In a process view, the exchange of meanings is incomplete without the judgement of the client on the accuracy of the counselor's understanding.

1.2.1. Whole-Person Process

The raw material of counseling is language. At the moment of mutual understanding, the three assumptions of the process model are operative: language is people; language is persons in contract; language is persons in response. Counseling consists of a series of contracts (cf. Egan, 1970, 26) which define the conditions, roles, and expectations of those involved. Conditions involved in the negotiations include the length, number, and purpose of the counseling sessions. All of these issues are discussed and agreed upon before the sessions are undertaken. At the beginning of each session, the general purpose and the time limit are clearly stated by the counselor. After he has established the basic contract, the counselor silently awaits the reaction of the client before proceeding further. The roles of the counselor and the client are defined by the contract. The task of the counselor is to provide a supportive and understanding milieu in which the client can discuss and solve his problems. The counselor does not give advice or impose solutions but assists the client in working out his own solutions. The client enters the relationship with the expectation of solving his problems or, at the least, achieving significant knowledge of himself and his living environment so as to improve his functioning as a person.

Both the counselor and the client are engaged in counseling as whole-persons. Their exchanges take place in both affective and cognitive language. From the linguistic viewpoint, language has been treated as a mere cognitive phenomenon consisting of messages. As whole-person process, language in its cognitive and affective aspects is a vehicle of learning, that is, of discovering interpersonal signification. The client learns from his own affects and from the counselor's understanding. The responsibility for learning lies with the client. The counselor provides the cognition which the client needs in order to solve his problems. The effect of the counselor's cognition is to set up a reflective process in the client. After the session, the client begins to reflect back on the session in order to grasp its meaning in more detail. As he accepts the responsibility for his problems, the client compares his experience in counseling with the experiences of his daily social relationships. From his experiences, he derives a new set of guidelines to behavior, a new set of values. When he grasps the significance of his actions outside the counseling hour, the client achieves better insight and control over his social environment. He learns to adjust his "investments" of himself in other persons and things (Curran, 1969, 40). Gradually, the client learns to reflect by himself, to construct his own inner world of reality, and to make the necessary social adjustments without the aid of a counselor. As Hiyakawa observes (1972, 21–33), the client symbolizes his world in "maps" which more realistically represent the "territory" in which he functions.

1.2.2. Educational Process

Education, according to Curran (1972), shares many features with whole-person task-oriented counseling. There are, however, two important differences between counseling and education. In counseling, affective language plays a dominant role. The focus of counseling is on the client and his problems – the basic reintegration of his affects with his cognition. The focus in education is upon cognition language. Affects play an important, but basically subordinate role in the educative process of achieving the mastery of an essentially cognitive task. Curran has written:

> If this seems at first surprising, it is perhaps because the emphasis on the understanding of the client in counseling-therapy, where he is primarily affective in his communication, has made us overconscious of the value of understanding the affective state. The importance of understanding the cognitive aspect that is also in the unified person has been overlooked (1972, 115).

A second difference between psychological counseling and education is the focus of the latter on a task. Curran (1972, 30) has stated that task-oriented counseling introduces into the educative process itself many of the subtleties of therapeutic and counseling relationships. Athletic and drama programs in schools in the United States have unwittingly and, perhaps, unconsciously, developed the subtleties of counseling-oriented education. In the task-oriented relationships, for example, of a football or basketball team struggling to achieve a successful season, one encounters many of the intense personal relationships that are encountered in task-oriented counseling relationships. The class play or other forms of dramatics which result in public presentation produce many of the same task-oriented counseling-learning dynamics. However, these have long been considered adjuncts to the educational program rather than central to it. A similar situation exists in the case of the Japanese school. In Chapter 3, the application of counseling-learning to the Japanese case with English language education will show how the educational process develops.

1.2.3. Interpersonal Process

Curran (1972, 29 & 33) has shown that counseling can be applied to education not only between individuals, but to groups as well. The teacher takes on the counseling role and the students form a group of clients. The application of counseling to second language acquisition is called "Community Language Learning." In the basic stages of learning, the teacher-counselor establishes the counseling—learning contract by announcing the time and the purpose of the session. Then he awaits the response of the students-clients before proceeding further. The foreign language class is introduced and treated as a counseling session as previously described. When an individual wishes to address the group, he uses the language of affect, ie, the native language of the learner. The counselor-teacher, in a supportive and empathetic way, states the message in the language of cognition, ie, the foreign language (called the "target language"). The learner slowly repeats the target language after the teacher. Each person who wishes to take part in the conversation uses the cognition language borrowed from the counselor-teacher to express what he desires to communicate to the group. The "conversation" is tape recorded and replayed for the group when the time limit is reached. A reflection session is also held in order to allow the student-clients time to evaluate their performance.

A different kind of social process occurs in the cases of those who have learned a foreign language through the linear or phrase structure models by memorizing basic sentence patterns, reading, translating, and so on. These students may even have been successful in passing academic and English proficiency examinations. However, just because of their cognitive proficiency, they may resent dependency on the counselor-teacher. They are unable to use a foreign language competently because of affective blocks preventing free expression and communication. In the Japanese case, students find themselves confused and anxious in the presence of a native speaker of a foreign language. Their cognitive "self" is well developed in the foreign language, but their affective "self" is retarded in its expression. This situation constitutes a serious counseling conflict for the learner. The counseling task is to reintegrate the cognitive self with the affective self in order to converse as a whole-person with a native speaker. The Japanese case with English is a fine example which will illustrate second language acquisition as social process. This will be the topic of later chapters of this book.

1.2.4. Developmental Process

The process view of language entails the constitution and growth of both the speaker and the listener. Curran has demonstrated the whole-person development of the client as he receives a broader understanding of his affects through the cognition supplied by the counselor. The counselor's skill also develops and increases as he becomes more and more sensitive to the communications received from the client. In its application to foreign language education, Curran (1976, 54) has claimed that the learner gives birth to a new self in the foreign language. The self grows through a five-stage developmental process from childhood (Stages I & II), through adolescence (Stages III & IV), to adulthood (Stage V). In Chapter 4, the growth process at each of the five stages will be explained in more detail as a cognitive task to be resolved and as a value to be enacted.

Apart from considering cognitive stages of the language development of children, linguists have paid little attention to language as developmental process. Along with the neglect of language as affect, certainly the dynamics of affective conflicts and their resolution in a language context are completely foreign to theoretical linguists. Of course, it is absolutely impossible to describe language development in terms of the acquisition and development of values. In just those areas most crucial to language as developmental process – affect, conflicts, and values – modern theoretical linguistics has failed to create a theoretical base for second language education.

1.2.5. Communicative Process

Some might argue that affects, conflicts and values lie beyond the scope of linguistics. But if we are to receive a complete concept of language which is pertinent to classroom practice, then affects, conflicts, and values must be seen as essential to language. Affects, conflicts and values need not be restricted to verbal modalities. The non-verbal is also language as communicative process. In counseling, the client's message is not restricted to the verbal order and includes psychosomatic attitudes, summarized by Curran as "Basic Emotive Instinctive Levels" (1969, 43). The client's communication of affects, conflicts and values may or may not correspond to his verbal message. While it is the counselor's task to help resolve the contradictions, he needs a more comprehensive view of language than traditional linguists have presented. Studies in non-verbal communication by Birdwhistell (1970), Sheflen (1974), and others are compatible with a process view of language. Other linguists have relegated this important facet of language to the edge of their field with the term "paralanguage." On this point, Crystal (1975, 163–4) has written:

> Paralanguage shares one thing with the study of other forms of body expression – namely, that it has been much neglected, even within linguistics. . . . There has been a generally dismissive attitude towards the study of paralinguistic phenomena in the context of communicative analysis – an attitude which is perhaps reinforced by the etymological conditioning of our thinking arising out of the 'para' prefix. There is the suggestion that tone of voice is a secondary facet of communication – a kind of optional 'extra,' which does not affect the basic meaning of an utterance.

Birdwhistell (1970, 48 and 49), taking a broader view of communicative process, has written:

> All kinesic research rests upon the assumption that, without the participants being necessarily aware of it, human beings are constantly engaged in adjustments to the presence and activities of other human beings. As sensitive organisms, they utilize their full sensory equipment in this adjustment. Any particular modality may have paramount definitional power in a particular communication situation, but these modalities may only be heuristically abstracted for study and

analysis. That is, although at any punctiform moment a person may be seen to be moving or vocalizing, the study of communicational scenes reveals that all the abstracted modalities are necessary to understand the communicational situation.

Another viewpoint in modern linguistics also clouds the issue confronting the teacher of foreign language. In spite of the fact that Chomsky (1972, 69, 70) has shown that human and animal communication are organized on entirely different principles, some linguists, such as Argyle (1975), still insist on presenting human communication as a more highly developed continuation of lower animal species. According to Argyle (1975, 6), most animal communication is merely a response to other animals. In contrast, Sheflen (1974, 12 and 29) reported a communicative process which included more than information transfer. He then took recordings and videotapes of a series of counseling-therapy sessions and worked through them with a group of anthropologists (Bateson and Birdwhistell), structural linguists (McQuown and Hockett) and process psychoanalysts (Fromm-Reichmann and Brosin). They observed much more to language and its kinesic infrasystems than the representation of some person, place, or thing by the use of words. A speaker will locate himself and orient his whole body to some other person or group. While he holds this basic bodily orientation, he may employ his head, eyes and speech in a sequence of lexical point units. He may also use his torso in a sequence of gesture points. He may use his upper body in a task performance, or he may simply orient his legs and/or his upper body to some person or subgroup, while he moves his head from one listener to another. However, the whole body is employed in a complex set of orientation and communicative activities. When this entire unit is completed, the speaker will shift his whole bodily placement or posture. Communicative processes of a non-verbal order will be taken up again in Chapters 5 (time) and 6 (silence).

1.2.6. Cultural Process

According to Crystal (1975, 162) an understanding of man's expressive potential requires the concurrent study of both linguistic and non-linguistic modes of behavior. Only a distorted picture can result from too rigid a separation between them. When we consider speech, it is paralanguage which is the man, as far as social identity is concerned (Crystal, 1975, 168). Therefore, linguists may no longer ignore non-verbal response because it is the communicative vehicle for cultural process. Barnlund (1975, 10) has written that the aim of human perception is to make the world intelligible so that it can be managed successfully. The attribution of meaning is a prerequisite to and a preparation for action. People are never passive receivers, merely absorbing events of obvious significance, but give an active response in assigning meaning to sensation. What any event acquires in the way of meaning appears to reflect a transaction between what is there to be seen and heard, and what the interpreter brings to it by way of response from past experience or prevailing motive. Thus, the attribution of meaning — the response — is always a creative process by which the raw data of sensation are transformed to fit the aims of the observer. Sheflen (1974, 45) has shown that representational behaviors are not universal in form and meaning; rather, they are culturally specific. When members sharing such forms come together to communicate a meaning, they use the same system of customary representational forms and thereby refer to a specific, culturally traditional set of meanings. Cultural process, therefore, is the creative group response of the learners. In the given instance of a short-term counseling session with CLL (Curran, 1972, 6), Japanese students provide a creative response according to their traditional norms and learning sets. The reflection period, which is traditional in Japan, greatly reinforces CLL learning activities. Reflection will be taken up in Chapter 7.

Others have treated culture as language (Hall, 1973), communication (Condon and Yousef, 1975), and social (Hirschmeier and Yui, 1981), or educational (Brooks, 1969) process. Halliday (1975, 139 and 140) has given us a thread which can serve to weave all the facts of culture together around the concept of a creative response. The social semiotic is the system of meanings that defines and constitutes the culture; and the linguistic system is one mode of realization of these meanings. The child's task in acquiring the first language, itself a counseling task, is to construct that system of meanings that represent his own model of social reality. This process takes place within the child's head; it is a cognitive process. But it takes place in the contexts of social interaction, and there is no way it can take place except within these contexts. As well as being a cognitive process, the learning of the mother tongue is also an interactive process. It takes the form of the continued exchange of meanings between the self and others. The act of meaning is the social act. The reality that the child constructs is that of his culture and subculture and the way in which he learns to build up registers — configurations of meanings associated with features of the social context — are those of his culture and subculture. In the Japanese case with CLL, learners of English do not hesitate to assert and defend their traditional learning sets in a strong and forceful way. In later chapters of this book, social learning sets called "culture learning mechanisms," an outgrowth of CLL contracts, will be identified and their use in the classroom will be described.

1.3. Summary

The purpose of this chapter, addressed to theoretical linguists and teachers of foreign languages, has been to introduce a teaching–learning model based on a social process view of language. In a process view, language is people, persons in contract, and persons in response. The following six qualities, derived from a process view of language, were developed: 1) whole-person process; 2) educational process; 3) interpersonal process; 4) developmental process; 5) communicative process; 6) cultural process. Part 1 was addressed to theoretical linguists. First, the social process view of language is different from the concept of language as communication. Second, other models by theoretical linguists have systematically eliminated essentials of the process model — person, contract, and response. Third, consideration of social constraints and interpersonal interaction can not be ignored if we are to develop an adequate theory of language. Part 2 was addressed to language teachers. The process view of language was shown at the moment of understanding in counseling. Whole-person process consists of the person in his cognition, his affects, his conflicts, and his values. Educational process is differentiated from counseling and the T-Group by the emphasis upon the cognitive task. Interpersonal process includes a simultaneous growth of cognition and affect. Through the developmental process, the learner is born and matures in five stages of social language learning. Studies in non-verbal communication are compatible with this model. Lastly, cultural process was described as creative group response. Each of the six qualities will be explored in later chapters.

Chapter 2
Whole-Person Process; The Research Methodology for This Book

2.0. Whole-Person Process

In Chapter 1 whole-person process was described from the point of view of the client. The purpose of this chapter is to focus on the person and values of the counselor-researcher. Science does not begin with the subject, but with personal change on the part of the scientist, a development in awareness and a deepening understanding of the subject. According to Polanyi (1974, 18), the scientific outlook is whole-person, as much emotional as intellectual. The expectations which it entertains are not mere idle guesses or hypotheses, but active hopes filled with enthusiasm. The emotions of the scientist also express and uphold the values guiding the research. The phenomena under study are not objects, but persons. In contrast to current research methodology, the crucial emphasis, according to Pratt and Tooley (1966, 885) is placed on "with" rather than "to" or "for" the subjects, whether individuals or groups. This means the negotiation of team contracts that are oriented toward co-actualization of all parties to the contract — professionals, clients, communities or publics.

2.1.0. Consensual Validation Research

Consensual validation research is a three-step process: group experience, reflection, and the formulation of tentative conclusions. Conclusions are based on group consensus and can be tested and reconfirmed or disproven after replication of the experience. The purpose of this section is to elaborate upon this simple formulation. Consensual validation is possible, given a psychological (research) contract between the scientist and the subject(s). A research methodology of participant-observation becomes the

17

field through which qualitative data are procured. Personal knowledge is gained through "indwelling" in the group phenomena (Polanyi, 1974, 142). Reflection results in a renegotiation of the contract by the scientist and the subject(s). The beliefs, judgement, and responsibility of the scientist are paramount in the interpretation and integration of the data in new and creative discovery. The rapidly growing research community of English teachers in Japan assists this process.

2.1.1. A Psychological Contract

A new set of relationships is needed if we are dealing with people, in order to handle interpersonal variables in a scientific way. Pratt and Tooley (1966) have argued for a unifying conceptual framework based on contract psychology that is sufficient to the human condition and the contemporary scene. In contrast to physical and mechanical models that dehumanize and demoralize man, they argue for concepts expressing freedom of choice and action, the human capacity for personal and social responsibility. From the perspective of contract psychology, the essence of human beings and their enterprises, of individuals and societies, is the capacity for the development and exchange of human values. Social relations represent contractual exchanges in the major spheres of living. Contracts are reciprocal agreements, promises, expectations, commitments, and covenants. Contracts are instrumentalities for the creation and exchange of human values. Team contracts useful for research purposes are concerned with the negotiated exchange of human values. The team contract, according to Pratt and Tooley (1966, 883), defines the team structure, team functioning (operational transactions), and team functions (purposes and goals). Contract conditions expressed or implied, formal or informal, represent the ends-means dimensions or attributes of the team and of all parties to team contracts – professionals, clients, consumers, and publics. But most important for research methodology, contract conditions also form the experimental conditions, treatment or predictor variables, for social-action research carried out by or about the team.

2.1.2. Participant-Observation

According to Maslow (1966, 78–79), science has a two-fold task. On the one hand, it must describe and accept the way things are, the actual world as it is, understandable or not, meaningful or not, explainable or not. Facts must come before theories. A scientist's first duty is to describe facts. On the other hand, science also presses steadily toward simplicity, unity, elegance, toward condensed, succinct, and abstract formulas describing the essence of reality, its skeletal structure, the ultimate to which it can be reduced. The good theory does both, or at least tries to. More accurately, it may be said, the good theorist does both and gets satisfaction from both kinds of success, especially if both come simultaneously. Systematizing and theorizing come after the facts. The first task of the scientist is to experience the subject. It is amazing how often this truism gets overlooked. For the scientist, his subject exists in the concrete world. The other world of theory, for instance, the world of the physicists and mathematicians, of abstraction, "laws," and formulas, of systems and postulates, is a world that is not directly experienced but rather rests upon the experiential world and is inferred from it. Theory is an effort to comprehend and understand the world and to make sense of it, to see behind its apparent contradictions, to order and structure it. The continuum from abstractness to simplicity can help us understand the activity of the researching teacher. In moving from the world of abstract theory to the concrete reality of the classroom the classroom teacher is closest to theory as it actually works in the concrete encounter with the students. Brown (1977, 274) has written:

> If teachers can think critically and follow some of the basic 'rules' of research, they can indeed engage in their own research projects in the interest of furthering the collective knowledge of the process of teaching and learning a foreign language.

We need research which leaves qualitative data intact, does not restrict the phenomena to mathematical terms, and which involves multiple data collection strategies based on participant-observation.

A form of participant-observation called "ethnographic research" has been described by Wolf and Tymitz (1977). Ethnographic research or ethnography is an analytic process involving the disciplined and systematic uncovering of human behavior and socio-cultural interactive patterns within any environment or milieu. It is imaginative and reconstructive, both ruminative and recollective. Research requires collection of data from a variety of sources, probing for the subtle and underlying meaning of the data, in the light of theory, at every step. The result is the interpretation of the phenomenon under study. This involves sustained interaction between the researcher and subjects within the culture, environment, or milieu under investigation. Such research employs techniques including: interviews, both structured and unstructured, retrospective and intro- spective; observation, both structured and unstructured; and does not necessarily exclude the use of statistical measures. The ultimate aim of these procedures is to provide accurate, detailed analysis of social settings. Ethnographic research involves the amassing of large quantities of evidence without testing preconceived hypotheses. Rather than large sampling techniques, the intensity of the exploration with even a few subjects is far more critical. In education, the careful probing to identify frames of reference relevant to both teacher and students is clearly more important than statistical treatment or display. It is essential to document, illuminate, and portray the layering of behaviors inherent in teacher—pupil interactions if one is to truly understand the nature of the learning process. The purpose would not be to test each of the subjects but rather to understand exactly what they do in relating to each other and how that facilitates instruction. Flexible and sustained observation and sensitive probing are necessary to clarify the complexity of the learning process. Understanding the context in which such interactions occur helps to clarify and modify emerging insights. The ethnographic paradigm provides a holistic perspective in which to integrate the multifaceted dimensions that remain disparate in the present research litany. The research yield is one that promises to be comprehensible to teachers and other practitioners not served by cryptic and esoteric presentations couched in statistical or mathematical language. Because ethnography relies more on natural language expressions, its capacity to link research and practice is greatly enhanced.

2.1.3. Knowledge by Indwelling

The scientific relationship can be based on a research contract between the scientist(s) and the subject(s). The scientist works on a continuum extending from the experience with concrete data to the abstract activity of constructing theory. This double activity undertaken by the scientist is his personal world; it forms a single "gestalt" with the person of the scientist at the center. Polanyi (1974, 89) described a gestalt of "personal knowledge" consisting of two different kinds of awareness: focal and subsidiary awareness. Although focal and subsidiary awareness are merged, we can pass from knowing what (focal awareness) to knowing how (subsidiary awareness) and note the similarities in the structure of both forms of knowledge. The difference between the two awarenesses is closely allied to another fundamental distinction, namely, between the parts of the body and things external to it. We attend to external objects by being subsidiarily aware of things happening within the body. When a person performs an activity, he has a focal awareness of that activity (such as driving a nail into a board), and a subsidiary awareness of the feelings from the body (from the palm and fingers as the nail goes into the board). Our subsidiary awareness can be regarded as a condition in which tools (Polanyi, 1974, 90) come to form a part of our body. We hardly ever attend to our body as intensely as we attend to an external object, although we continually rely on it as a means for observing and manipulating objects for our own purposes. We may identify, therefore, our knowledge of something through attention to something else with the kind of knowledge we have of our own body by dwelling in it. In other words, we may say that when we rely on our awareness of some things for attending to other things, we have assimilated these things into our body. We may say, for example, that we know the clues of perception by dwelling in them. When we attend to that which they jointly indicate, we see the whole by dwelling in the parts. We thus arrive at the conception of knowing by indwelling.

Indwelling operates on all levels of reality. The process may be generalized to include the acceptance and use of intellectual tools such as are offered by an interpretive framework – a theory – and, in particular, the formalism of a science. While we rely on formalism, it is not an object under examination, but a tool of observation. We adhere to it only as long as it serves a useful purpose, until it can be discarded for something better. Science does not require that we study man and society in a detached manner (Polanyi, 1974, 96). On the contrary, the part played by personal knowledge in science suggests that the science of man should rely on greatly extended uses of personal knowledge. When we know living things, our indwelling enters into an especially intimate relation to that which it knows. The perception of living beings consists throughout in mentally duplicating the active coordinations performed by their living functions. We can see now how we know another's mind and share his mental life.

Knowing a man's mind is to experience the joint meaning of his actions by dwelling in them from outside. This is how we get to feel another man's consciousness, to share his pain and pity him. Knowing life is always a sharing of life, but to know another person is to share his life as an equal partner. That is why we need a contract between partners to govern the relationship between the researcher and the subject(s). When we study inanimate matter or the lower organisms, we stand to these in an I–It relationship, but as we gradually rise to the study of man, we arrive at an I–Thou relation to him. We enter into a mutual understanding with him based on a scientific contract. The theory of knowledge by indwelling accounts for the personal knowledge of the scientist in its abstractness and in its concrete form of experience.

2.1.4. Reflection

We also need a research methodology based upon a form of knowledge other than experience to formulate scientific principles and interpret the meaning of raw data. This form of knowledge involves the beliefs, the judgement, and the responsibility of the scientist for his work. Besides the world of experience, the scientist dwells in the abstract task of formulating his conclusions. In this sense, he dwells in reflection. Knowledge can be gained through reflection based on renegotiation of the contract, ethical principles, and the advice of the scientific community.

(a) Renegotiation. According to Pratt and Tooley (1966, 883), the time is long overdue for renegotiating team contracts. Radical revision of team contract conditions would provide for the reconceptualization of the nature of the problems to be dealt with; of team tasks; of team organizational structure, duties, privileges, obligations, and of the accountability of all parties to the contract. This means renegotiation among team members themselves, between teamsters and other professionals, and between team professionals and clients, consumers or publics. Von Eckartsberg (1973, 288) has called for cooperative dialogue between scientists and person-subject informants. The researcher enters into a give-and-take with the person he studies. If the researcher establishes negotiation, he can compare and contrast his own observations with those reported by the person studied. The feedback function provides a two-way change process. Not only does the subject receive valuable feedback from the researcher, the researcher also obtains valuable knowledge clarifying his observations from the person studied. Both the person researched as well as the research-person are thus being changed through a research dialogue based on a mutual contract. They change each other. As Pratt and Tooley have written (1966, 226):

> As a reflexive open-contract system (subject to periodic renegotiation) the actualization team can exploit feedback and also change itself, its contractual context, and its own social role. This provides for ongoing, progressive actualization of the team as constructive change agent.

(b) Beliefs. Reflection involves a formulation of tentative conclusions on the part of the scientist. Roozeboom (1970, 226) has claimed that the primary aim of a scientific experiment is not to precipitate decisions, but to make an appropriate adjustment in the degree to which one accepts, or believes, the hypothesis being tested. As researchers, it is our professional obligation to work from available data to explanations and generalizations, ie, beliefs, supported by the data. But belief in (acceptance of) a proposition is not an all-or-nothing affair; rather it is a matter of degree. The extent to which a person believes or accepts a proposition translates pragmatically into the extent to which he is willing to commit himself to the behavioral adjustments prescribed by the proposition. While the researcher must indeed make decisions, his science is a systematized body of probable knowledge, not an accumulation of decisions. The end product of a scientific investigation is a degree of confidence in a set of propositions which then constitutes a basis for decisions.

(c) Responsibility. Ethical issues in scientific research have long occupied the attention of psychologists. As far as TESOL is concerned, our studies with human subjects, especially in personal and delicate areas such as affective counseling and cultural values, have not touched on the ethics surrounding scientific judgement. In 1973, the American Psychological Association published a code of ethics for the conduct of research with human subjects. The first principle states:

In planning a study, the investigator has the responsibility to make a careful evaluation of its ethical acceptability, taking into account these principles for research with human beings. To the extent that this appraisal, weighing scientific and human values, suggests a deviation from any principle, the investigator incurs an increasingly serious obligation to seek ethical advice and to observe more stringent safeguards to protect the rights of the human research participant.

The judgement of a TESOL researcher with regard to the human research subjects as yet remains unguided by a code of ethics. However, the judgement of a scientific researcher can be guided and assisted by the scientific community.

2.1.5. Summer Workshops

Contacts with a scientific community greatly stimulate interest, awaken new ideas, and serve as a guide to research. The TESOL community has grown around summer workshops sponsored by public and private organizations. One of the most outstanding in Japan is the summer workshop for Japanese teachers of English held at the Language Institute of Japan in Odawara. This workshop has grown into a busy intersection where various lines of research cross and provide mutual influence. Community Language Learning, the Silent Way, English through Drama and many other methods have all been represented. Other workshops are sponsored by the Prefecture and City Boards of Education. Teachers with eight or nine years of teaching experience are given a chance to refresh their skills during summer vacations. Universities also provide workshops or sponsor special lectures for representatives of different fields. These workshops are especially valuable because they provide a forum where new ideas are readily received and put into immediate practice. Feedback from professional teachers serves as a guide for further study.

2.2. Summary

Consensual validation research is the negotiation and communication of values occurring in interpersonal relationships of the scientist and his subjects, with his colleagues, and with the larger scientific world. According to Bixenstine (1976, 52), living in company with others is impossible unless allowance is made for non-consensuality. When we differ, but must carry on nonetheless, we resort to a favorite human invention — the contract. So important is the contract in realizing human values that it is often confused with value. Contract formulation is a valued human enterprise preferable to the anarchy which reigns in its absence. But the need for contracts arises because people respond to an event with different values. Contracts are our way of creating consensus. Contracts are not contrary to fact, rather they start with fact and proceed to embrace a wider scope of experience and understanding. They enable persons of different values to live and communicate, if not in the same world, then at least in permissive proximity.

Chapter 3
Socio-culturally Oriented Education

3.0 Introduction

A social pedagogy based on a counseling contract is effective in dealing with learning difficulties, especially those encountered in second language acquisition. One such social pedagogy is called Community Language Learning (hereafter: CLL). If CLL were to be applied without due consideration for the group dynamics already operative among the learners, the results would be the same or even less effective than current methodologies now in vogue. However, CLL, in conjunction with the group dynamics operative among the learners in any given society, is a more effective way of dealing with the difficulties of the learners. Given the open counseling situation as described in Chapter 1, the learners react according to the norms of their culture. These norms can be adapted to CLL contracts called "culture learning mechanisms" (Chapters 9 and 10). Examples from the Japanese case include the age-hierarchy and reflection. These will be considered here only briefly. The focus of this chapter will be on the characteristics, applications, and the results of a living psychological contract. By way of convenience, English language learning, so active in Japan, is the medium through which socio-culturally oriented education is exemplified.

Current methods of learning foreign language, based on behavioristic psychology (Esper, 1968; Elliot, 1972), suffer from serious defects. First, learning is seen as merely a cognitive process without consideration for the affects and conflicts of the learners (Curran, 1968, 295). Second, serious defects in the pattern practice hypothesis have been shown in both the language laboratory (Lindsay, 1973) and in the classroom (Corbluth, 1974; Stevick, 1974). Foreign language is not learned only by memorizing or repeating intellectualized patterns. The creative use of language is also crucial in the learning process. Third, according to Bradford (1970, 75), there are important goals in language learning that have been relegated to secondary position in behavioristic methodology. These goals, which are

26

concerned with the psychological, sociological, and cultural experience of learning, form the psychological contract that develops in the dynamic relationships of a group.

PART 1: THE CHARACTERISTICS OF THE LIVING PSYCHOLOGICAL CONTRACT

3.1.0. Counseling-Learning

In place of behavioristic learning in which, for instance, second language acquisition is viewed as a mere repetitive intellectual process, Curran (1972, 11) developed "Counseling-Learning" in which the need goals (Egan, 1970, 77) of the learner are handled in a dynamic social process. Learning is a unified personal, social, and contractual experience that bestows special worth on the learner. It is unified in the sense that the whole person is involved in learning – not simply intellect and memory. The student is engaged in a deep social experience bound by the rules of a contract. He no longer learns in isolation or in competition with others, but in and through them. The rules of the contract experience operate in a living way to resolve affective problems and conflicts. Therefore, Curran used the term "Counseling-Learning."

3.1.1. CLL

The special application of counseling learning to foreign language education is called CLL. Although a specialized application of Counseling-Learning, CLL is general enough as a psychological contract to embrace the social learning mechanisms operative in any culture. CLL may be defined as follows: CLL is a supportive language contract which consists of group experience and reflection. There are five elements of this definition which are important for a proper understanding of CLL: first, CLL is a learning contract; second, CLL is supportive learning; third, CLL is group experience; fourth, CLL is group reflection; fifth, CLL is language learning.

3.1.2. Community

CLL is a learning contract. A contract is an agreement by a number of individuals to engage in a common task for the purpose of achieving some goal. In contrast to isolated learning which occurs in language laboratory booths, CLL learning occurs in groups. But CLL suggests more than a large learning group. Curran (1972, 30) purposely adopted the term "Community" instead of "Group" language learning. A group is composed of a number of people engaged in a common task. A community is formed around a contract (Curran, 1976, 50–51). The existence of an interpersonal contract differentiates CLL from forms of group learning suggested by others, for example, Byrne (1976, 280–2). The term community is intended to introduce, in addition, the intense self-involved dynamics that a common group contract implies. Interaction, role, and dedication are also included within the scope of the term "Community." The interaction is governed by a series of social rules which make the group cooperative and give it direction (cf. Egan, 1970, 26–27). The interaction of a large group with the participation of the teacher (Type I) stems from a different set of rules than a small (Type II) or pair group (Type III) learning experience. Community also means a change of roles. The teacher can alter his role in a flexible way and implement any of the three kinds of experience over the course of a semester in order to meet the changing needs of the students. As will be shown later (Chapter 6), the teacher operates on a dynamic interpersonal continuum from activity (Type I) to partial (Type III) and even total silence (Type II). The role of the students also changes as they gain confidence and independence (Stevick, 1976b, 126) in speaking a foreign language.

At any point in the life of the community, the social rules can be isolated and identified during a period of review, which is included in the term "Contract." The dedication of individuals – the amount and quality of English spoken – can be evaluated by the teacher and students together in a reflection period. The existence of a reflection period as part of the contract differentiates CLL in a unique way from mere group activity. This characteristic of CLL is also part of Japanese culture. Every social organization in Japan will hold a period of reflection as part of its on-going activity. Group reflection is viewed as essential to the smooth functioning of any social activity. Group learning activities can also fit into the scope of CLL as "subcontracts." Activities such as role playing, oral composition, and discussions are evaluated by the students during a reflection period. Thus, CLL dynamics are centered around sociological, psychological, and cultural

experiences in learning – a psychological contract – which in the behavioristic view are termed "secondary" goals of learning.

3.1.3. Learner Space

CLL is supportive learning. Supportive learning derives from the way
"Learner Space" (Curran, 1972, 91–96) is used by the teacher. Because of
the knower's greater knowledge and other differences such as age, life
experience, nationality, personality characteristics and so on, there exists
a difference or space between himself and the learners. This space is necessary if one person is to learn from another. But if the knower projects himself into that space, allowing no room in it for the learner, he destroys any
opportunity for the learner to expand into it.

When the teacher provides learner space in a supportive way, the learner
develops according to the norms of his native culture. In the Japanese case,
learner space is provided for the dynamic functioning of such culture
mechanisms as the age hierarchy and reflection. The contract relationship
to the teacher becomes similar to that of a pre-Meiji period Japanese school
(Dore, 1965) or in the small private schools (juku) which still flourish
outside the regular school system in modern Japan. Traditionally, the
teacher allowed learning to take place through free interaction among the
pupils themselves. However, he was not so distant from the individual as to
defeat the learning process. He also delegated responsibility to those more
advanced for the education of those less advanced. Teacher and students
together formed a living learning community that Curran (1972, 28) has
called a "Discipline." The CLL discipline is not only the subject learned,
but the whole personal learning experience itself. It implies an internalizing
of what has been learned and the self-control necessary to bring about
understanding in the person himself.

Learner space is used in another supportive way. Type I, II, and III
learning experiences are time-limited. The time limit frames the learner
space within the bounds of a contract agreement. This reduces the anxiety
in the interpersonal dynamics of the class. Because they can accept a time-
limited experience with less anxiety, the learning activity is placed closer
to the grasp of the students.

3.1.4. Short-term Counseling

CLL is group experience. In English classes as we know them, the action of the teacher fills the learner space completely. The learning occurs on a single interpersonal dimension between the teacher and the whole class. The evaluation is handled by the teacher in the form of tests and examinations. This kind of education has been called "teacher-centered." By way of contrast, the task of the CLL teacher is to build many more communication bridges across the learner space within three basic interpersonal dimensions. In common with teacher-centered methods, the first dimension is between the teacher and the whole group. However, the teacher does not monopolize the learner space. He establishes, for example, a "short-term counseling session" (Curran, 1972, 5) of about ten or fifteen minutes. In short-term counseling, the teacher sets up a brief, time-limited group learning experience. He explains the purpose of the activity and clarifies the time limits but he does not suggest topics for discussion or force the response of the students. The teacher awaits the reaction of the students and supports their efforts to build a conversation. His supportive silence during a Type I experience reinforces "student-centered" learning. The second interpersonal dimension is between the teacher and individuals in the class. A Type III experience in pair or triad groups allows the optional participation of the teacher, as will be shown later. The third interpersonal dimension is between the students themselves. Besides the need for learning with the participation of the teacher, students have a need to develop their skills independently. They do this by teaching each other. Besides the interpersonal space between the teacher and students, there exists a distance between the students themselves. Curran (1972, 94) has said of this space:

> It is the task of the teacher-knower, therefore, to recognize the space not only between himself and the learners, but also between the learners themselves, some of whom may not understand the subject matter as clearly and completely as others.

A Type II experience affords the students a chance to bridge the differences and variations in their behavior among themselves. They perform this task by exchanging and sharing their information in a supportive way even though the teacher does not participate in the learning experience. The CLL teacher reinforces the Type II activity by his supportive silence.

3.1.5. Reflection

CLL is group reflection. At the end of every CLL session, time is provided to reflect upon the experience of the day. Students are allowed to comment upon the experience as it relates to the individual student and the teacher. The untapped areas of the experience are the dynamics at work in a particular group in a particular culture. The CLL reflection period is open in a special way to the Japanese cultural mechanism of reflection and to the dynamic operation of silence. If silence occurs during the experience part of the CLL session, its meaning will be pursued during the reflection period. Contract, interaction, process, content, and need goals are also reviewed in the living dynamics of the group. Events of the experience are examined (content goals), together with the way in which they were carried out (process goals). The problems and motivation (contract and need goals) of the students as well as those of the teacher (interaction goals) come up for discussion during CLL reflection periods. Accommodations in the group contract can be made in such a way that the learning goals of the group are emphasized.

3.1.6. Hierarchical Growth

CLL is language learning. Curran (1972, 123–35) compared development in language proficiency to the birth and growth of a new self in language learning. He proposed five hierarchical stages of growth in language learning from the perfect dependency of childhood to the independence of the adult stage. These five stages will be described in detail in the next chapter. They are mentioned here as an example of socio-culture in education. The CLL hierarchy corresponds to the culture mechanism of the Japanese age hierarchy (Nakane, 1970, 26) where the younger (kohai) learns from the older (sempai). In Stage I, the embryonic stage, the younger (kohai) is given birth and is completely dependent upon the teacher and the older (sempai) for anything he wants to say in the foreign language. The younger speaks in the language of affect (Chapter 1.2.2), his native language. As he begins to pick up the language, the younger moves up the hierarchy into Stage II (the self-assertion stage) and III (the separate existence stage). When the younger moves from childhood to adolescence as a foreign language speaker, he begins to use simple phrases independently.

Increasingly, the younger picks up expressions that he has heard from others on his own horizontal social level or from the older on a vertical social level. In Stage III, the younger begins to function in the foreign language without the use of the native language. As the learner's capacity unfolds, he needs to assert his own unique way of speaking the foreign language in a strong and forceful manner. The counselor and the sempai must be aware of this and accept it as inherent in the language learning process if the younger is to be helped at this stage.

Stage IV (the reversal stage) represents a crucial transition in the learning relationship. It might be considered a kind of adolescence. If the younger is to acquire further refinements in the foreign language, he must begin to create an atmosphere of understanding and acceptance for the teacher and the older. The roles have to be interchanged. The younger has to understand the counselor and the older in their need to teach. Otherwise, the older, out of fear of offending the younger, tends to become increasingly hesitant about giving further knowledge of the foreign language. The burden of the psychological understanding shifts to the younger. He must make it possible for the older to communicate refined knowledge of the foreign language.

In Stage V (the independent stage) the younger theoretically knows all that the older has to teach. Although the younger is independent, he may still need subtle refinements and corrections. The younger is now able to become a sempai to the younger members of the group who are less proficient. During the course of his activity in counseling, the older still receives further correction from the teacher.

PART 2: THE APPLICATION OF THE LIVING PSYCHOLOGICAL CONTRACT

3.2.0. An Experiment

The purpose of Part 2 is to describe an experiment and the dynamics that occurred in the class group when CLL was introduced. Culture mechanisms such as reflection and the age hierarchy were fully exploited in CLL as it was applied in the Japanese case. The experiment showed that CLL applied with a pertinent culture learning mechanism (reflection) afforded a flexible social situation in which foreign language learning could occur. The focus of group activity was the mastery of a foreign language, in this case English.

3.2.1. Subjects

The experiment was initiated in formal language learning groups in a typical classroom setting. The subjects were female students of Nanzan Junior College (age 20–21). Conversation classes included thirty to forty students, some of whom were only part-time students of English. Because of their previous six years of English study they were able to read, but not to converse freely. They were fully competent to answer any examination question about English grammar. The experiment as described here continued for two years, 1973–75.

3.2.2. Four Obstacles

The contemporary foreign-language learning class, as a social entity, presents four serious obstacles to learning: a) in the student–teacher relationship; b) in the relationships among the students; c) in the social milieu; d) in the contract.

a) Oral drilling, according to Corbluth (1974), is an obstacle to learning and may even be harmful, especially for intermediate and advanced students. With mechanical drilling, liveliness and interest quickly give way to fatigue and boredom. What students need (Corbluth, 1974, 124) is a wide and deep experience of English in use. Furthermore, knowledge of the language is dispensed by oral drilling performed only by the teacher. As a social process, language learning takes place on a single vertical dimension from teacher to students. The value of this type of teacher-centered language teaching has been called into question by Stevick (1974).

b) Obstacles to learning also exist in the relationships among students. In secondary education, the students have to study for tests, which in contemporary Japan means stiff competitive university examinations. These examinations, hitherto equated with foreign language learning, are graded on a curve that pits students against each other in bitter competition. For the sake of a higher grade on a learning curve, students become winners or losers in a learning game. Stevick (1974, 11–13) has given a fuller description of the language learning game. Other students suffer anxiety in the competition and, fearing failure and rejection, become apathetic and are inclined to withdraw from learning. In the class, little attention is given to the needs of students for a shared group experience free from competition or for a supportive type of learning that is communicated on a horizontal interactional dimension from student to student.

c) Disharmony in the class milieu results from differences in motivations. Some students develop a fairly high commitment to learning, but others seek to escape from as much learning as possible. Essentially, some members of the class are at war with others. The teacher spends much time and energy keeping the dissonant parts of the class in some degree of harmony. Differences gradually take on the form of social forces that may serve to protect the less committed students and punish those who show some zeal in learning. Bradford (1970, 74) has described the social dynamics of the modern classroom as follows:

> Needless struggle takes place between teacher and student as to who shall learn and what; desirable concomitant learning goals are not realized; and students build barriers to present and future learning and frequently end up with lasting anxieties and undesirable attitudes toward education.

d) The fourth obstacle to learning is the lack of a "Contract." The motives and expectations of those who engage in the form of social activity called education are simply not discussed as part of the learning process. Students are questioned about their motives only as an afterthought, if they are performing poorly in class or on examinations. The teacher's motives for proposing class activities are never questioned or even discussed.

The teacher enters the class with the expectation that the students will grasp every activity which he proposes. If the students do not grasp the activity, the teacher becomes discouraged and even angry. His expectations of the class have not been fulfilled in the social relationship. If the students do not learn the language, they too become discouraged, because their goals for learning have not been met. Because neither the expectations of the teacher nor those of the students are realized in the class learning relationship, both end up frustrated and angry. One of the main difficulties of the class is that the motives, the goals and the expectations of the students and teacher are not discussed in their language learning relationship. In short, there is no forum for a discussion of the language learning contract in the class.

3.2.3. Learner Space

When CLL was introduced into formal instruction, learner space was provided within the mechanisms of Japanese culture. In order to avoid the competitive learning situation of the class, examinations were eliminated. School requirements were satisfied by the substitution of periodic reports in place of tests. Since the students were all the same age and sex, the Japanese age-hierarchy was not overtly functional in the social dynamics of the class groups. However, in place of the age hierarchy, other culture mechanisms such as reflection and silence were operative in a crucial way.

3.2.4. CLL Reflection

For instance, learner space afforded the student a chance to review the CLL language speaking experience during a period of reflection at the end of each class. The student's handling of silence had reference to her motivation in learning and her attitude toward the class. If the student remained silent during the CLL speaking experience in violation of the group contract, the explanation of her conduct was given during the reflection period. These explanations seemed to follow a cultural pattern which is more amply explained in Chapter 7.

3.2.5. Four Developments

Reflection was especially crucial in four areas of the social relationships among the class members: a) a great amount of anxiety in the presence of the teacher; b) a demand for independence from the teacher; c) a need for contact with the teacher; d) greater security in the presence of the teacher. The four developments took place as an on-going learning relationship between the teacher and students and among the students themselves. They defined the nexus of the social dynamics of the class.

a) The first development of CLL in the Japanese classroom confirmed a theoretical axiom of Curran (1968, 295):

Any discussion of the educative process has really to start with the relationship of conflict, hostility, anger, and anxiety to learning.

In previous research with CLL at the University of Michigan, a group of Spanish speaking adults reacted with great hostility to the introduction of CLL. The hostility conflict was resolved through a counseling dialogue with the students in which reflection played a vital role. In contrast, the Japanese students, perhaps because of the absence of an age-hierarchy, reacted with a great amount of anxiety. However, as in the Spanish group, reflection played a crucial part in the resolution of the anxiety conflict.

Because of their previous British education, the students had learned many English words and sentences, but they lacked basic communication ability to deal with another person, especially a foreigner. The students were caught in the dilemma of an anxiety conflict. On the one hand, they wanted the opportunity for free English speaking afforded by a CLL group; on the other hand, their anxiety in an unstructured situation was so great that they could not speak. In the absence of the age hierarchy, they had no social structure in which to operate and, as individuals, they had no confidence in themselves as speakers of English. Brown (1973, 233) has recently suggested that self-confidence and self-identity could have everything to do with success in learning a language. Any language acquisition process that results in meaningful learning for communication may involve some degree of identity conflict regardless of age and motivation of the learners.

For the purpose of bringing about a psychological birth process in CLL Stage I, learner space was provided so that individuals could gain confidence and identity as English learners through activity in supportive small groups. The purpose of these exercises, such as self-introduction, group questions and answers, statements and reactions, was to give the students a basic experience of CLL foreign language speaking. The anxiety conflict was discussed during the reflection periods. When the students realized that anxiety was a common problem, they assured each other by word and action that the threat did not really exist. Actions took the form of expressing interest in each other's learning progress, praising the efforts of those who broke the silence first, and expressing public gratitude to those who were most active during the foreign language speaking experience. In this way, reflection was crucial in resolving the anxiety crisis as the students progressed through CLL Stages I and II.

b) Reflection also brought home to the students the fact that the horizontal dimension of the social interaction was not sufficient for significant advance in language learning. This realization arose in connection with further developments in the social dynamics of the class. With growth in self-confidence came the demand for independence as a second development in the group dynamics. Contact with the teacher was accepted with reluctance. Preference for the security of the small group persisted. As the students showed signs of self-assertion and the desire for a separate existence in CLL Stages II and III, the teacher withdrew from the class activity. The students were allowed to speak English in small groups by themselves. They were able to progress by using the English they had previously learned. A variety of topics, freely chosen by the students, were discussed in the small groups.

c) The third development was the group's need for contact with the teacher. During the reflection periods after the small group activity, the psychological contract came under discussion. As evidence of Stage IV learning became apparent, the students realized that some understanding of the role of the teacher was necessary if they were to make further progress themselves. First of all, contact with the teacher was cut off. English mistakes were repeated. Worse still, English was spoken, at the most, about 80 percent of the time spent in the small groups. If progress was to be made in English, contact with the teacher had to be re-established even at some cost in effort.

In order to meet the need of the students for contact with the teacher, the class divided into larger units of ten to fifteen students for a Type I experience. A ten-minute period of free English conversation was held with each group. The role of the teacher, who was present in the group, was to show the students how to struggle with the problems of anxiety and silence. The teacher suggested that the silence could be broken by asking another person a simple question or by relating some incident which happened since the last class. The students were left free to decide which of these suggestions to develop in the independence of CLL Stages III, IV, and V. In response, the students accepted the responsibility for the content of the conversations and struggled together to make the time a useful English-speaking experience.

d) The next development was greater security in the presence of the teacher. The threat of the large group activity diminished during the discussions which took place in the reflection periods. Once the anxiety was shared by all the members of the class, it quickly evaporated. The supportive communication among the students gave rise to a greater understanding of the helpful role of the teacher. By this time, the role reversal of Stage IV had taken place. The students seemed prepared for Stage V practice, the one-to-one English speaking relationship, a CLL Type III experience.

PART 3: RESULTS AND DISCUSSION

3.3.0. Results

Results of the experiment showed that: a) a learning atmosphere combining CLL together with Japanese cultural mechanisms was conducive to second language acquisition; b) the anxiety characteristic of Japanese speakers can be handled in a supportive learning milieu; c) even silence can contribute to second language acquisition; and d) socio-learning becomes centered on values.

3.3.1. Socio-culture Learning

First, the learning atmosphere of the CLL class was conducive to second language acquisition. The social atmosphere of the class compared favorably, according to the students, to that of a Japanese temple festival (Matsuri). Students also felt rather startled by the realistic communication of the CLL class groups. Because the social interaction goals allowed free exchange in different kinds of large and small groups, they were able to become acquainted with each other. This was especially true of the pair groups where the interaction goal became a value within easy reach. In contrast to other foreign-language classes in which activities are carried on either in isolation or in single, rigid, monolithic units, the CLL class allowed the individual to meet and communicate with many other students. Consequently, as an interaction value, they were able to develop more creative relationships among themselves in the CLL class than in other oral English classes. This finding is especially significant in the light of Lindsay's (1973, 6) criticism of language learning laboratories:

For some students there are serious psychological drawbacks in being isolated from the teacher and other students. They need the face-to-face relationships and stimulus of group work. Moreover, for most students there is the need to transfer correct language behavior from the Lab to the realistic communication of the classroom.

3.3.2. Operation Understanding

Second, anxiety which is characteristic of Japanese speakers can be handled in a supportive learning atmosphere. During the experiment, the students grew so confident of themselves as to be able to handle a difference of opinion with their teacher in a constructive way. "Operation Understanding" arose from a difference of opinion between the students, who desired a fixed topic for each class, and the teacher who refused the request. A compromise was worked out in the reflection periods. Each student was asked to draw up a list of interesting topics, for example, hobbies, travel, friends, marriage, and so on. A single topic for each class was discussed in small groups. The discussion was summarized and reported to another group. The other group had to repeat back the message. The new form of activity, called "Operation Understanding," encouraged listening and communications skills, important facets of foreign language learning. Since students were put in charge of the class discussion, the needs of the junior college students for a share in the responsibility for the class were fulfilled. In this way, the need goals of the students were transformed into need values operant in the CLL social milieu.

3.3.3. Silence

Third, even silence can contribute to language learning. During the experiment, students were both shocked and stimulated into action by the realization of the damaging effects of silence on their progress in foreign language, especially when silence occurred in violation of the contract during CLL free conversation sessions. However unsympathetic a teacher might be towards the less motivated, a strong stimulus to action was provided during the reflection periods by a simple apology: "I am very sorry that you have lost your opportunity to progress by remaining silent. Since the time for free conversation has passed, the opportunity is gone and it can't be brought back." When the realization of irretrievable loss was brought home to the students by way of reflection, the silent blow was worse than any form of verbal or corporal punishment. In this way, the cultural mechanism of silence became functional as a process value which unified the CLL experience and reflection periods as the group pursued its goal. Socio-cultural silence will be the subject of Chapter 6.

3.3.4. Values

Fourth, the group process leads to socio-culture learning which, according to Bradford (1970, 81), becomes centered on values. However, in the Japanese case, cultural mechanisms are central to the process. The Japanese case with CLL demonstrates that, in the social dynamics, contract goals are transformed through the cultural mechanisms into contract values. Interaction goals become functional as interaction values. Process and need goals become process and need values. CLL together with cultural mechanisms (in the Japanese case, age-hierarchy, reflection, silence, and others to be introduced in Chapter 9) form the psychological contract. Foreign language learning is focused on social values to be sought after in community. Bradford (1970, 82), one of the originators of the T-Group, says that these values are most easily learned through the shared experiences of a class group and are not learned by imposition from the teacher, but experimentally from the trials and tribulations of the class group as the values are diagnosed openly by all. Value-oriented learning can accrue for any group regardless of subject matter (Bradford, 1970, 82) if the group is systematically built and if it takes the responsibility for uncovering and solving its learning difficulties.

Chapter 4
The Epigenetic Principle in Community Language Learning

4.0.

Erik Erikson (1959, 52) used the term "Epigenetic Principle" in reference to human growth. The epigenetic principle states four conditions of human development: first, people grow; second, people grow in sequence; third, people grow in time; fourth, people grow together in community. The purpose of this chapter is to focus on the epigenetic principle in Community Language Learning (hereafter CLL). A proper understanding of the epigenetic principle will assist foreign language teachers to identify the reactions of individuals and the changes which occur in CLL groups. The ability to place the reactions of students in some theoretical frame of reference will also be helpful to those who have had little experience in counseling and group dynamics. Appropriate CLL contracts can then be designed for students at different levels of growth. Knowledge of the epigenetic or growth principle in CLL will facilitate the planning of activities both inside and outside the classroom.

The epigenetic principle and its application to CLL will be explained in Parts 1 and 2. An epigenetic chart for second language learning, based on the growth principle, will be presented in Part 3. This diagram is introduced with two restrictions. First, it is meant primarily for Japanese students of English conversation, though reference to other foreign languages will be discussed. Second, the epigenetic diagram is restricted to CLL and does not apply to other forms of foreign language learning. Although the scope of the epigenetic diagram is restricted to CLL, it is hoped that focus on the epigenetic principle in CLL may become a reference point for understanding growth in foreign language acquisition regardless of teaching– learning methods.

41

PART 1: THE EPIGENETIC PRINCIPLE

4.1.0.

The purpose of Part 1 is to explain the epigenetic principle, which states four conditions of human development. The first condition is that people grow. According to Erikson (1959, 52), anything that grows has a ground plan, and out of the ground plan, the parts arise. Each part has its time of ascendency until all the parts have arisen to form a functioning whole. At birth, the baby leaves the chemical exchange of the womb for the social exchange system of society, where gradually increasing capacities over a period of time meet the opportunities and limitations of the culture. Personality develops according to steps predetermined in the human organism's readiness to be driven towards, to be made aware of, and to interact with a widening social radius. Awareness begins with the dim image of a mother and ends with mankind, or, at any rate, that segment which "counts" in the particular individual's life.

Second, people grow in sequence. Erikson (1959, 53) says that growth in sequence indicates, first, that each skill of the healthy personality is systematically related to all others and that they depend on the proper development in the proper sequence of each item. Second, growth indicates that each item exists in some form before 'its' decisive and critical time normally arrives. In the case of a child, Erikson (1959, 54) provided the example of an emerging form of autonomy in the first year of life. At age two or three, the growing child's concern with autonomy attains the proportions of an affective crisis. After the crisis, a more mature form of autonomy appears in the fourth or fifth year. It is important to realize that in the sequence of the child's most personal experiences, the healthy child, given a reasonable amount of guidance, can be trusted to obey inner laws of development, laws which create a succession of potentialities for significant interaction with those who tend the child. While such inter-action varies from culture to culture, growth must remain within the proper rate and proper sequence. Growth includes the achievement of a number of cognitive tasks and skills.

Third, people grow in time. Sequence and time are closely connected in human growth. In order to express the time component of the child's physical and social growth in the family, Erikson (1959, 54) employed an

"Epigenetic Diagram." An epigenetic diagram formalizes a differentiation of parts through time. The diagrammatic statement is meant to express a number of fundamental relations that exist between the components, for example, between the acquisition of a cognitive skill and the affective conflict at each stage of development. The social value to be exercised at each stage also has a relationship to the cognitive skill and the affective conflict. Within each stage of growth, the person must face a decisive encounter with the social environment. The social environment, in turn, conveys to the individual its particular demands, decisively contributing to the character, the efficiency, and the health of the person in his culture. The decisive encounter consists of an affective crisis; he may fail to achieve the cognitive task. As a result, the growth of the whole organism may be slowed or stopped completely. If the person resolves the crisis, he accomplishes the cognitive task and emerges strongly from a lower to the next higher stage of development.

Fourth, people grow together. The human being, at all times, from the first kick in the womb to the last breath, is organized into groupings of geographic and historical coherence: family, class, community, nation. He becomes an adult through learning experiences from which are derived values. Values act as a guide to behavior and seldom appear in a pure or abstracted form. The social conditions under which behavior is guided, in which values work, typically involve conflicting demands, a weighing and balancing, and the result is an action that reflects a multitude of forces. Complicated judgements are involved, and what is really valued is reflected in the outcome of life as it is lived. Values, therefore, are related to the experiences that shape and test them. They are not, for any one person, so much hard-and-fast verities as they are the results of hammering out a style of life in a certain set of surroundings. Certain things are treated as right or desirable or worthy. These tend to become our values (Raths *et al.*, 1966, 28). If values become rigid, development stops. Affective crises are resolved through continuing exercise of values in a community.

PART 2: THE EPIGENETIC PRINCIPLE IN CLL

4.2.0.

The purpose of Part 2 is to show how the epigenetic principle applies to

CLL. First, the epigenetic principle states that people grow. CLL is whole-person growth in language. Besides the intellect, affects and values are involved in learning. The beginner must struggle through a series of conflicts which involve his personal development in the new language. The ground plan for growth in language consists of five stages. The first two stages reflect the experience of childhood. The learner is totally dependent upon the knower for anything he wishes to say in the foreign language. The second and third stages represent a transition from the total dependence of childhood to the partial dependence of the adolescent. Stages 4 and 5 are like the transition from adolescence to adulthood in the foreign language.

Second, the epigenetic principle states that people grow in sequence. The existence of a sequence among the cognitive tasks of second language learning is a matter of controversy. The sequence of cognitive tasks as summarized by Curran (1972, 136–7) will be presented later in this section. The cognitive tasks are creative. Through membership in a CLL group, the learner gradually constructs a grammar of the foreign language.

Third, people grow in time. When faced with a new cognitive task, the learner must also solve an affective crisis. With the solution of the five affective crises, one for each CLL stage, the student progresses from a lower to a higher stage of development.

Fourth, people grow together in community. CLL growth takes place in a supportive community; that is, students learn by helping each other in supportive group experiences. A community is distinguished by a number of members in different roles, a learning goal, and a psychological contract. The psychological contract consists of a supportive group learning experience together with its reflection period. The contract is flexible enough to permit the teacher to adopt either an active or a silent role during the participation in CLL learning. The role of the students also changes as they develop greater proficiency in the foreign language.

The reflection period is of vital importance in CLL. During the reflection period, the learners review their performance during the experience. They rate their actions and progress toward the goal for better or worse. On the basis of these reflections, they form resolutions for performance during subsequent CLL sessions. These resolutions are guides to behavior which are hammered out after a group learning experience. The content of the reflection is reported and shared with others in the group. With the help of these guides or values, the learners meet and solve their affective conflicts.

The cognitive tasks of foreign language learning are accomplished through the struggle. There are five values which are conducive to group learning and should be fostered by the teacher at each CLL learning stage.

In the next section, the relationships between the affective conflicts and values will be explained at each CLL stage. Appropriate CLL contracts will also be suggested. The epigenetic principle in CLL applies to each component through the five stages. The mastery of cognitive content is a creative growth process. If instructors could only be convinced that ideas also have to grow, we would witness some significant changes in the teaching of grammar. The solution of five affective conflicts through the exercise of five values is also a developmental process. The remainder of this section will be devoted to a more detailed explanation of growth in foreign language through five stages together with the cognitive tasks of each stage.

4.2.1. Five Stages of Language Learning

In accordance with the epigenetic principle, CLL is the birth and growth of the whole-person in foreign language. Curran (1972, 128–41) has distinguished five stages of growth from childhood (Stages I & II) through adolescence (Stages III & IV) to adulthood (Stage V). In Stage I, the "Embryonic Stage," the learner is completely dependent upon the knower for linguistic content. In a group of five people, the "existent" people communicating in the group are A, B, C, D, and E. The "non-existent" people in the group are A_1, B_1, C_1, D_1, and E_1. When a learner decides to address the group, he speaks in his native language and native self as A. The counselor, who repeats the message of learner A in the target language, assumes the role of A_1. Then learner A speaks to the group in as close an imitation of the sounds coming from A_1 as possible. A_1 is the new self of the learner which receives existence, is generated or born, in the target language. Since the other members of the group overhear the communication between A and A_1, Curran (1972, 130) has called this dialogue an "Overhear." The result of the overhear is that every member of the group can understand what Learner A is trying to communicate. Likewise, if Learner B wishes to address the group, B speaks to the group in the native language. B_1 (the counselor) repeats the message in the target language. The message in the target language is repeated by Learner B. In the exchange with the teacher a moment of understanding has occurred. Although the student may have parroted the target language, upon reflection he achieves knowledge. The student has made the first step by taking responsibility for the task of learning. Through the overhear, the learner is given birth in Stage I and begins to grow in the target language with the assistance of the counselor. The figure of a nurturing parent is the analogy employed for the help and support which are provided by the counselor in Stage I.

In Stage II, the "Self-assertion Stage," the child achieves a measure of independence from the parent. Members of a CLL group begin to use simple phrases on their own with great personal satisfaction. They pick up expressions which they have heard and employ them as the beginning of their own self-affirmation and independence.

Stage III is called the "Separate Existence Stage." Individuals in the group learn to understand the other members directly in the foreign language. Use of the native language drops off during Stage III. The learner also begins to resent any assistance which the counselor would like to provide, especially when he or she offers knowledge which the learner already possesses. The end of Stage III can be thought to correspond to the child's learning to walk.

Stages II and III are preambles to Stage IV, called the "Reversal Stage." The child begins to express himself quite independently of the parent— knower. He communicates by himself unless he "stumbles," or needs help. The learner undergoes a transformation into independence in the foreign language. This means that he will be making fewer mistakes, will need less help as he is more securely able to communicate on his own.

Stage IV represents a crucial transition in the knower—learner relationship. It might be considered a kind of adolescence. As the learner grows in independence, the knower's assistance is increasingly rejected. If the rejection of the knower becomes complete, the relationship will be prematurely terminated. Although the learner functions independently, his knowledge of the foreign language is still at a rudimentary level. In order to achieve a more appropriate social level of refinement in the foreign language, the learner must still rely on the knowledge of the knower. During Stages I, II, and III, the knower has performed the understanding role in the relationship. In Stage IV, the burden of psychological understanding shifts to the learners. They must make it possible for the knower to communicate the advanced level of knowledge that he possesses.

Stage V is called the "Independent Stage." Theoretically, the learner knows all that the knower has to teach. Although the language may be independent, he may need some subtle linguistic refinements and correction. It is at this stage that the student should refine his understanding of register, ie, the distinction between correct usage of the foreign language and situationally appropriate language. The student in Stage V can become a counselor to less advanced learners. As the learner fulfills a counseling role in assisting others, he can still profit from contact with the knower.

4.2.2. Five Cognitive Tasks

The second condition of human growth is sequence. In CLL, there is a cognitive task for each of the five stages of growth. The cognitive task of Stage I is the construction of basic grammar or the application of one's previous learning to the social situation at hand. In the Japanese case, a distinction must be made between adult learners of English and adult learners of other foreign languages. With foreign languages other than English, the tasks of the learner are to apprehend the sound system, assign fundamental meanings, and construct a basic grammar of the foreign language. The overhear, defined by Curran, is applicable to this group of tasks. After several months (or about eight sessions) of CLL activities at Nanzan Junior College, a small group of students were able to learn the basic sound and grammatical patterns of German.

The Japanese case with English on the adult level, which, very broadly speaking, includes university students and businessmen, presents a very different phenomenon. Because of their previous acquaintance with English for six years of secondary education, the Curran overhear is unnecessary. But because their English has been memorized as a cognitive exercise, the state of their English may be considered "fossilized," as described by Vigil and Oller (1976, 281). Fossilization occurs when the second language acquisition is non-simultaneous with the acquisition of a child's first language, and also when it occurs in the absence of native-speaking peers of the foreign language. Fossilization may also occur because of unresolved affective conflicts which accompany the presentation of foreign language. Japanese students exhibit unresolved affective problems left over from their first English study. The counseling task of the English teacher is to design and promote learning activities which encourage supportive inter-action in groups. The task of the Japanese learner of English at Stage I is to apply the knowledge which he or she already possesses in order to function in an English-speaking social environment.

The cognitive task in Stages II and III is the construction of an "Inter-language." Interlanguage is a term first used by Selinker (1974, 117) to express the existence of a separate linguistic system which results from a learner's attempted production of a target language norm. The term is used here to denote the learner's ability to express affective meaning in a creative way, even though the cognitive form does not achieve the standard norm of the target language. Selinker used the term in a very broad way to include the whole range of production from the basic phonological stages to the proficiency of an adult native speaker. Interlanguage is used here in a more restrictive sense than Selinker's, referring to intermediate levels of ability at CLL Stages II and III. During Stage II, interlanguage is used in connection with the native language. Therefore, the cognitive task of Stage II is called "Interlanguage I." The student begins to express himself directly in the foreign language without using the native language during Stage III. Since the expression in the target language does not yet meet the standard norm and is still semigrammatical, the term "Interlanguage II" is used for the cognitive task of Stage III. Since the two tasks, Interlanguage I and Interlanguage II, are similar, and the learners are continually advancing in foreign language and falling back into the native language as they struggle to advance again, the distinction sometimes becomes blurred in practice. Progress in foreign language takes place in a very erratic way during Stages II and III. The semigrammatical expression of meaning in the first three CLL stages is important for the learner in order to cope with his affective conflicts. The teacher's intervention to correct mistakes is inappropriate during Stages I, II, and III.

In Stage IV, the task of the learner is the analysis of his own errors. Richards (1974) has defined error analysis as:

> The field of error analysis may be defined as dealing with the difference between the way people learning a language speak, and the way adult native speakers of the language use the language (p. 32).

The role of the learner in Stage IV is to use the language in the presence of the teacher. The learner is aware that he may make mistakes and can be led to correct them by a hint from the teacher. If the mistakes are simple, they can be corrected by the learner. If they are more fundamental or involve the use of new forms, then the teacher's intervention is necessary and welcomed. The reason for this change of attitude on the part of the student will be explained in Part 3.

The task of Stage V is to learn appropriate social use of the target language. Under the direction of the teacher, the learner exercises a counseling function in the group. He gives help to the less advanced when they call for it. At Stage V, the teacher demonstrates more appropriate social uses of the foreign language, if the learner requests it. Since the learner at Stage V functions at near-native level, the teacher may find it unnecessary to intervene. By this time, his or her interlanguage has changed through the analysis of errors to a point where the learner has achieved the standard norms of the target language.

PART 3: AN EPIGENETIC DIAGRAM FOR COMMUNITY LANGUAGE LEARNING

4.3.0.

The purpose of Part 3 is to explain the epigenetic diagram for CLL. The first two components of the diagram, namely the five stages of language learning and the cognitive tasks of each stage, have already been presented. The connection between a cognitive task, an affective conflict, and a value will be explained at each CLL stage.

4.3.1. Stage I

The cognitive task at Stage I is to apply the knowledge of English to meet the social demands at the moment of use. This task is accompanied by a great amount of anxiety which blocks the expression of English, especially in the presence of a teacher or native speaker of English. Evidence from a training course for English teachers shows that even after years of English study, Japanese learners may be so petrified by anxiety that they are unable to speak or even hear when confronted with an English speaking

Stages of growth	Cognitive tasks	Affective conflicts	Values	CLL contracts
Stage I (Embryonic)	Construction-application	Anxiety	Courage (Self-confidence)	Short-term counseling
Stage II (Self-assertion)	Inter-language I	Identity	Cooperation	Culture mechanisms (Self-introduction)
Stage III (Separate-existence)	Inter-language II	Indignation	Docility	Values clarification
Stage IV (Reversal)	Error analysis	Role	Trust	Short-term counseling
Stage V (Independent)	Appropriate social use	Responsibility	Leadership	Culture mechanisms (Club-workshop)

An Epigenetic Diagram for Community Language Learning

situation. In Stage I, the counselor must help the client to identify the affective conflict which prevents him from speaking English. This can be accomplished through a short-term counseling session (Curran, 1972, 5). At the beginning, the teacher clearly announces the type of activity and the time limit, usually ten minutes. The teacher then silently awaits the students' response. There is usually a long period of silence and a great amount of anxiety. Japanese members may force certain individuals who are considered more proficient to speak as representatives for the whole group. The teacher should observe the time limit very strictly and the reflection period should begin promptly after the speaking experience has ended. If the students are given a chance to think about the speaking experience and to write down their reflections, some of the anxiety will disappear. The two problems, anxiety and silence, are readily identified during the reflection period. The teacher can point out the connection between them. They were silent because they were anxious. The connection may be apparent to the teacher, but the students may not be so aware that their reactions to silence touch their basic motivation in learning English. Learning a foreign language is a difficult task. People need courage in order to face and overcome their anxiety. Through the exercise of courage, the students face their anxiety and learn to apply the English which they know to meet the demands of the social situation. The value of courage contributes to a more fluent cognitive expression of English. The problem of silence is more simple. If everyone makes an effort to speak, the silence very quickly vanishes.

4.3.2. Stage II

By encouraging mutual assistance in the face of anxiety, the teacher has prepared the students for cooperation with others, which is the value for Stage II. By this time, the students have received a greater degree of insight into the condition of their English. During senior high school, they have learned a great many words and memorized many English grammar rules which are more or less correct. In Stage II, the English learner begins to use his interlanguage to find an identity as a speaker of English. "Identity" is a term used by Erikson to express an individual's link with the unique values of a group. Erikson (1959) has explained the term as follows:

> The term identity expresses such a mutual relation in that it connotes both a persistent sameness within one's self (self-sameness) and a persistent sharing of some essential character with others (p. 102).

The persistent character to be shared and sought after in a CLL group is a goal, namely English speaking. Consequently, small group contracts based on native customs and culture will be very helpful for learners at Stage II. Self-introduction is a fine example in the Japanese case. Other examples of these "Culture Learning Mechanisms" will be more fully explained in Chapter 9. In Stage II, the teacher assumes a silent role by designing activities which allow the students ample use of interlanguage in small groups, even though there is danger that the English is semigrammatical and the use of Japanese cannot be excluded.

4.3.3. Stage III

The use of the native language gradually drops off during Stage III. However, this development goes hand in hand with another crisis. The students find great satisfaction in the creative use of the English which they have already learned. Apart from the teacher in their small groups, they achieve a sense of security which also becomes an obstacle to progress. However, three problems are reported during the reflection periods: first, the students become more and more aware of deficiencies in the grammatical quality of their English, but no one corrects their mistakes; second, it is difficult to learn new forms and constructions in the small groups; third, the students find themselves speaking their own language in their small groups. The presence of the teacher is needed to stimulate conversation in English.

The values of Stages I and II — increased self-confidence, courage, and cooperation — have contributed to greater fluency and security in English speaking, but the learning has occurred apart from the teacher. If the values of Stages I and II become rigid, they become obstacles to further progress. The relationship with the teacher must be re-established toward the end of Stage III. Curran (1972, 132) has described the affective crisis of Stage III as follows:

> A strong force for learning in these latter stages is an affective one, specifically, indignation. As the learner's capacity to learn unfolds, he often needs to assert his own unique way of learning in a strong, forceful manner. The knower must accept this as inherent in the learning process if he is to help the learner . . . Such personal indignation is a necessary assertion on the part of the learners, indicating that they do not wish to stay in the previous stages of dependency. Once they have 'grown up' they feel indignant when they are not allowed to exercise the independence that their increased knowledge gives them. It is the task of the counselors to help them by accepting them in their anger and willingly withdraw unnecessary aid.

The contracts for Stage III consist of clarification of the values and issues operative in the group. Suitable exercises can be found in Simon, Howe, and Kirschenbaum (1972/1978), Hawley and Hawley (1975), and have also been suggested by Davis and Keitges (1979). Self-evaluation can also be built into the CLL reflection period. Ask the students to state, in terms of percentage, the amount of English and the amount of their native language used during their small group activities. The rationale for their conduct makes the students aware of the real issues involved in the teacher's silence during the small group discussion. Either the teacher must be allowed to perform a helpful role, or else the class will degenerate into a picnic without learning a thing. Acceptance of the teacher is vital to the group at the end of Stage III. But first, the students must also accept themselves as imperfect speakers of English if they are to receive help from the teacher. The inability to solve the affective crisis of indignation leaves the English of many students in an underdeveloped cognitive state at Stage III. The reason is not lack of knowledge of the cognitive rules of English, but an affective inability to accept one's self as an imperfect learner in need of assistance from another. The simple ability to be a learner, called "docility" by Curran (1972, 49), solves the crisis of indignation at Stage III.

4.3.4. Stage IV

Acceptance of self and the teacher leads to mutual trust. The exercise of trust leads to the solution of an affective crisis about the role of the teacher and the learners in Stage IV. During the first three stages, the teacher has performed the role of understanding the learners. At Stage IV, the learners begin to take over this role. With the growth of trust, the teacher can be completely at ease because, by this time, the learners have overcome the initial anxiety of Stage I. They have achieved a commitment to learning through the exercise of courage and cooperation in working together with others. The teacher is freed by the understanding and trust of the students to perform the necessary tasks of analyzing and correcting errors. The indignation of Stage III gradually changes into a constructive force for independence.

The epigenetic principle can be exemplified by comparing the performance of the same students during a short-term counseling session at Stage I and at Stage IV. At Stage I, the short-term counseling session is characterized by the painful experiences of anxiety and silence. Participation in the conversation is limited to one or two students who have been pushed into the leadership position by the other members of the group. At Stage IV, everyone participates in the lively conversation and there are few pauses or silences. Responsibility for the topic is shared by the whole group. Because of the increase of confidence and trust between the teacher and students, the errors which crop up can be quickly corrected without interrupting the flow of the conversation. Role reversal is also evident during the session. The student becomes alive and active in his English self, but perfectly silent in his Japanese self. As a native speaker, the teacher is silent in the English self, but active in the Japanese self. During short-term counseling sessions at Stage IV, I have found myself speaking Japanese while giving grammatical directions, pointing out new constructions and correcting mistakes. During these sessions, I felt less like an English teacher and more like a referee at a football game.

4.3.5. Stage V

Theoretically, the learner at Stage V has mastered all the knower has to teach. However, knowledge of appropriate social use can be further refined at Stage V. For this purpose, responsibility is the best teacher. The knower can share the responsibility of counseling with those who by age or proficiency have achieved greater independence than the other members of the group. In Japan this can be done with a group of senior high school or university students in an English-speaking club. The teacher deals only with the leaders of the group at the top level of the Japanese age hierarchy. The leaders of the group carry out their counseling function in assisting the younger members.

The delegation of responsibility by the teacher precipitates a crisis of responsibility. The acceptance of responsibility by an emerging leader or leadership group is accompanied by anxiety which can be handled through individual counseling. The leader must be presented with clear alternatives among a choice of proposals. If necessary, the consequences of each choice should be clarified, but the final choice should be left to the leader or to the leadership group. Clarification of the issues and roles involved in carrying out a decision is sufficient to dissipate the anxiety which arises. As the leader performs his counseling function, a more refined level of English use becomes noticeable. The leadership that emerges is characterized by the giving of self, by listening to others, and by providing necessary assistance. The giving of self means using time and energy for different projects. The emerging leader follows the teacher's example in listening from below. The level of English which is handled by a fellow student is often clearer to a younger student than the explanation of the teacher. The teacher adopts a silent role in Stage V. He intervenes only to provide more appropriate usage. The silence of the teacher greatly reinforces the activity of the emerging leader. One of Curran's students has written (1972, 157):

This gives me a profound confidence that when sentence after sentence receives only the warm support of silence and an approving symbolization, I am again deeply strengthened in my secure identification with an adequate French self. For me it has been a striking experience in how the warm con-validation for someone you completely trust can be so confirmed in an area of knowledge.

PART 4: SUMMARY AND CONCLUSIONS

This chapter has concentrated on the nature and application of the epigenetic principle in CLL. The nature of the epigenetic principle was explained in Part 1, and its application in Part 2. An epigenetic diagram for CLL was then presented. Whole-person growth is the accomplishment of cognitive tasks, the solution of affective conflicts, and the respect for the enactment of values. English teachers can promote the development of an interculturally oriented leadership if, in the language learning context, teachers help learners to face themselves, accept their own limitations, and be open to the limitations of others. In the language learning context, values such as courage, cooperation, docility, and trust promote the development of a leadership that is capable of intercultural communication.

Chapter 5

Seven Clocks: Their Ailments and Their Realignment

5.0

According to Hall (1973, 1), time talks. Time speaks more plainly than words. Because time is manipulated less consciously than other messages, it is subject to less distortion than the spoken message. An understanding of the non-verbal dimension of time in teaching–learning is necessary for any educator no matter what he teaches. Hall (1976, 2) has forcefully written:

> The future depends on man's transcending the limits of individual cultures. To do so, however, he must first recognize and accept the multiple hidden dimensions of the non-verbal side of life.

The purpose of this chapter is to explore the hidden and unstated messages of time which influence the progress of classroom learning, to look at the problems these messages cause, and to discover solutions to these problems through CLL.

The clock analogy was used previously by Joos (1967) as a "linguistic excursion into the five styles of English usage." Joos employed the clock analogy in order to state five principles concerning first language use. First, Joos recognized the complex way in which a native speaker adjusts his language to the various social contexts in which he speaks. Second, Joos saw that the repetitive nature of the linguistic adjustments could be described in specific and systematic terms by the clock comparison. Third, the linguistic clock has alarms. Joos observed that grammatical usage is connected with negative affective reactions such as guilt when a speaker deviates from accepted norms (Central Standard Time). Fourth, the members of the same language community share the same clock and know how to read its messages. Grammatical usage serves to define an individual as a member or non-member. Joos (1967, 8) wrote:

> Beneath their cant, the members of the community are unconsciously familiar with those other values: that is, in fact, what it means to 'be a member of' a community. The unaware familiarity is what makes the values effective and gives the individual his profit from them.

Fifth, Joos stressed the fact that the learner built and adjusted the clocks for himself with more hindrance than help from schooling.

If accommodated and applied to second-language acquisition, the five principles of Joos will help us to understand the time messages we are sending to our students in class. The first three principles of the clock analogy will be applied in Part 1. In the classroom, students of a second language adjust their conduct to time messages from interpersonal learning contexts (Principle one). If we examine the interpersonal context, not five, but at least seven clocks are ticking away in our classes. Our awareness of the covert messages being received and sent is, at present, minimal (Principle two). Three of the clocks are not even under the control of the teacher. The cultural clock, the social clock and the semester clock stem from the context of the historical age and the time limitations under which we work. Although we might not be able to alter them, we can become more aware of their effects and attempt to alleviate any detrimental messages sent to the students. Something can be done, however, to alter the messages of the other four clocks, the communicative clock, the student clock, the developmental clock, and the teacher clock. As they operate in our classrooms, the seven clocks are in disarray and, consequently, our students are receiving confused messages. The negative effects of the repetitious messages will be formulated in terms of a problem with each clock, and an "alarm bell" when the problem causes a more acute obstacle to learning (Principle three).

The last two principles of the clock metaphor will be applied in Part 2. The student of a second language has to acquire the values of another community which operates within a different time framework. This means that the learner has to acquire the skill of sending and receiving not only the correct, but also the appropriate message at the right time (Principle four). While the learner is struggling to acquire the linguistic skills necessary for functioning in a new community, an inner time clock of the new world must be constructed by the learner himself and not merely imposed by the teacher (Principle five). The teacher of a second language can be greatly assisted by a time-related learning mechanism called SARD (a cryptonym referring to six elements of CLL, namely, Security, Attention-Aggression, Retention-Reflection, and Discrimination). The problems outlined in Part 1 will be addressed and solutions within the time framework of the SARD mechanism will be suggested. SARD works like a key which realigns the seven clocks. When all the clocks are functioning in harmony, the result is a consistent message, an appeal for dedication to the difficult task of learning a foreign language. Even if CLL is not employed, the key is available to any teacher who can use it to deepen awareness of the influence of time upon learning.

PART 1: SEVEN CLOCKS AND THEIR AILMENTS

5.1.1. The Cultural Clock

The first clock is the cultural clock. The cultural clock refers to the basic attitudes of a people toward time. All societies allot time according to a set of underlying values which evoke commitment when the time schedule is followed or resistance when it is broken. According to Kluckhohn (1971, 348), all societies at all times must deal with three time problems. All have some conception of the past, all have a present, and all give some kind of attention to the future dimension. They differ, however, in their emphasis on these time periods. American attitudes toward time tend to be oriented toward the future, whereas Spanish-Americans tend to emphasize the present. In Japan, the present and the past are both emphasized, while in China, more emphasis is placed on the past. Consequently, if cultural clocks from these two.language backgrounds are ticking away in the classroom, there is bound to be a clash from the underlying values connected with time. In a more general way, the problem being posed by the cultural clock might be formulated as follows: How are differences in values reconciled in the classroom?

In this connection, Hall (1976, 7) has distinguished between "monochromatic" and "polychromatic" time systems. Americans generally operate on monochromatic time; that is, they prefer to do one thing at a time, requiring one kind of implicit or explicit scheduling. Latin-Americans tend to follow polychromatic time schedules which allow for many events to occur together. Japanese, on the other hand, operate in both mono-chromatic and polychromatic ways. Time is subject to negotiation. The Japanese are willing to wait and allow a decision to emerge when the time is ripe. Until the whole group is ready to make a decision together, many different kinds of activities will be occurring in a polychromatic way. But once the decision is reached by common and unanimous consensus, the time system becomes rigidly monochromatic. The schedule will be carried out in a very mechanical way. The Japanese group will even become self-critical if the schedule is not carried out exactly as decided beforehand. A more specific problem with reference to Japanese culture might be posed as follows: How does the teacher schedule activities so as to accommodate both monochromatic and polychromatic time systems in the classroom? Because of the close relationship in attitudes between time and values, the influence of the cultural clock can not be underestimated. In its most powerful function, it produces all the other clocks. The social, semester, and communicative clocks are all products of the cultural clock. Even the reaction of the teacher, student, and developmental clocks are dictated to a great extent by the cultural clock. Clark has written:

> One's consciousness is inextricably bound up in the unconscious network of ideas, opinions, and presuppositions that one brings to any social encounter. For most people, this reality is never questioned nor even, perhaps, recognized as potentially different from reality as perceived by others (1976, 384).

5.1.2. The Social Clock

The social clock relates to the world outside the classroom. In the social world, time is divided in a variety of ways by the rotation of the earth around the sun, by the rotation of the moon around the earth, or, in a popular way, by the changes in climate and season. The seasonal calendar with its summer, winter, spring, and fall brings social events which lure the interests of our students. The progress of learning inside the classroom is influenced by the turn of social events outside. The problem posed by the social clock is how to relate the events of the classroom to the social demands of the real world outside.

5.1.3. The Semester Clock

Most language learning takes place today in the context of a school, which is a time-learning arrangement devised arbitrarily by modern culture. The "school year" is divided into two or three semesters, or into four quarters. The semester, in turn, is divided into a number of days and class hours. At the base of all this is the pure fiction of the "credit hour." The semester clock is set with an alarm bell which sounds out the time for examinations. After the examinations, the "evaluation" occurs in terms of low or high grades on a competitive scale. The problem posed by the semester clock is how to build a learning community in such a competitive system.

5.1.4. The Communicative Clock

The communicative clock designates an important task already described by Joos (1967) in reference to first language acquisition. The native speaker shifts from one style of speaking to another, like the hands of the clock, with each ticking social environment. However, the communicative clock ticking away in our second language classroom has become stuck because of our reliance upon grammar, textbook materials, and on the analytic aspects of teaching and learning. The textbook has been organized into units which fit into the requirements of the semester clock rather than the needs of the learner of the foreign language. With the advent of values clarification and discourse analysis, we are beginning to see a welcome change. Discourse analysis, according to Larsen-Freeman (1977, 173–4), is a linguistic methodology which looks at the semantic and communicative functions of language, structural unity at the suprasentential level, the input to the learner, and the input/output interaction. *First*, the student learns how to converse, *then* how to interact verbally. Out of these inter-actions, the grammatical structures grow and develop. This is the exact opposite of the chronological events of most of our classrooms which proceed from textbook to social interaction. If educators could only see that analytic structures and ideas also have to grow and mature, we would see some significant changes in the teaching of grammar. However, though textbooks based on values clarification contain series of exercises for social interaction, they contain no pattern practice sentences for memorization and are, therefore, difficult to use. Thus, the problem remains: How does the learner acquire the flexibility to shift his style of speaking, as a native speaker does, with each change in the social environment?

5.1.5. The Student Clock

The student clock refers to the presence and participation of the students in class. The participation of the students can be compared to a clock which has two hands indicating physical and psychological presence. Psychological presence means interest and dedication to the tasks of learning. The student clock is sensitive to alarm bells which stem from the semester and teacher clocks. If the alarms signal loudly and cause a high level of anxiety, then the hands of the student clock move rapidly from psychological to physical presence. The expressions often heard from the students themselves are, "He shut me off," or, "I got turned on." The student may be physically present in the classroom, but his interests and dedication follow directions outside the classroom dictated by the social and cultural clocks. Without any reàl investment in learning, the student may operate to defeat the system and make it through school with a minimum of effort. The problem for the teacher is to involve the students in classroom activities.

5.1.6. The Developmental Clock

The developmental clock refers to the inner needs of a learner for personal development in learning together with others. Ideally, the student and developmental clocks should be fused in whole-person learning. Because of the overemphasis on the analytic process of memorizing and repeating sentence patterns, the developmental clock suffers from neglect and runs in a confused way. From the viewpoint of the student, one message is read (and likely to be followed) on the cultural and social clocks while the semester clock encourages competition with others on a grading scale. The teacher may suggest that the students use English in class, then proceed to fill the gap caused by the students' silence with lengthy explanations of the grammar and phraseology of the foreign language. The confusion of the clocks contributes further to the inefficient functioning of students in class. Realignment of the clocks is made more difficult because of another value difference in relation to time. Because their concentration span is brief and many conflicting social and cultural events compete for their available time, students tend to observe polychromatic time schedules. Teachers, on the other hand, present a more limited scope of activities and fairly narrow goals. Teachers operate on monochromatic time schedules. Consequently, the problem posed by the developmental clock remains: How can we promote the personal development of the learner within the foreign language classroom?

5.1.7. The Teacher Clock

The teacher clock is generally more attuned to the semester clock and its requirements than to the student or developmental clocks. The teacher steps into the classroom with a lesson plan that might be a number of pages from a textbook to be taught in any given hour. If there is no feedback or response from the students, the lesson plan becomes nothing more than an arbitrarily devised time-learning schedule which is blindly imposed on the students. Such a schedule might be necessary for the younger learners, but the resistance which develops from adult learners of college age and beyond may become counterproductive to learning. Periodic quizzes and examinations on the teacher clock function like an alarm system, producing anxiety in students. In this way, the teacher clock requires physical presence, but not necessarily psychological presence. The students must also meet the semester clock's requirements. If the teacher were more attuned to the developmental clock of the students, lesson plans would not be based on the completion of tasks within a given time but on students' needs. The serious problem presented by the teacher clock is: If the teacher has no definite plan or syllabus to follow, then what is the function of the teacher?

5.1.8. Eight Questions

Thus the seven clocks have posed serious questions for the teacher: First, how are differences in values reconciled in the classroom? Second, how does the teacher schedule class activities so as to accommodate both monochromatic and polychromatic time systems? Third, how can we relate the events of the classroom to the social demands of the real world outside? Fourth, how can we build a learning community in the competitive situation produced by the semester clock? Fifth, how can we help students learn to shift communicative styles according to changing social situations? Sixth, how can we get students not only physically but psychologically involved in classroom activities? Seventh, how can we promote the students' personal development within the language classroom? And, eighth, if we give up the traditional lesson plan, what is the function of the teacher? The answers to these eight questions, or at least the way they are handled within CLL, is the subject of Part 2.

PART 2: THE REALIGNMENT OF THE SEVEN CLOCKS

5.2.0. Commitment Mechanisms

As was pointed out in the introduction (Principle four), the student of a second language has to acquire the linguistic values of another community operating within a different time framework. The function of the teacher (question eight) is to assist the learner in this task by using what Kanter (1972) called "Commitment Mechanisms." Commitment mechanisms are specific ways of ordering and defining the existence of a group. Examples of commitment mechanisms are property, work, social boundaries, recruitment, group control, leadership and ideology. These diverse pieces of social organization can be arranged to promote collective unity, and provide a sense of belonging and meaning to the members of a group.

> These issues can be summarized as one of commitment, that is, they reflect how the members become committed to the community's work, to its values and to each other, how much of their former independence they are willing to suspend in the interests of the group. Committed members work hard, participate actively, derive love and affection from the communal group, and believe strongly in what the group stands for (Kanter, 1972, 65).

The CLL teacher fosters dedication to learning through a system of commitment mechanisms called "SARD," which stand for Security, Attention-Aggression, Reflection-Retention, and Discrimination. SARD is made up of repetitive contractual units which lead to self-investment. First, SARD is made up of units which are incomplete in themselves. At the base of SARD is a psychological contract which consists of a learning experience together with its reflection period. The experience may be very broadly applied to include any kind of group learning activity such as listening, speaking, reading, writing, and so on. In addition to experience, the SARD mechanism includes reflection as essential to learning. Both experience and reflection, when employed in the context of group learning, provide a learning system whose timetable is determined by the needs of the learner. As was pointed out in the introduction, the learner constructs and adjusts his own inner clock as he adopts the time system of another language (Principle five).

Second, the SARD mechanism repeats itself again and again like a clock mechanism. The repetition allows the teacher to use time in either a polychromatic or a monochromatic way, as will be shown later. The careful monitoring of the students' affective reactions leads to a discussion of mutual interests. The flexibility of the SARD system enables the CLL teacher to plan activities which the teacher has decided are necessary or to implement activities which have been suggested by the students during reflection periods. Differences in values can then be negotiated as part of the learning contract (question one). The result, in the fourth place, is a consistent appeal to the students for self-investment in learning.

Lastly, the students gradually assume some responsibility for the smooth functioning of the class community. The SARD system works like a key which brings order into the disjointed elements of time which characterize our classrooms. The remaining problems of Part 1 will be addressed within the SARD framework.

5.2.1. Security

The problem posed by both the cultural and semester clocks is how to develop a supportive atmosphere in the classroom beset with potential cross-cultural misunderstanding and the anxiety of competition. According to Stevick (1977, 19), the first task of the teacher is to establish relative security, a security in which the students are able to function with responsibility for their own learning (question eight). The security of the students is never absolute; otherwise no learning would occur. A further distinction can be made between interpersonal and cultural security. Interpersonal security refers to the supportive atmosphere among the participants fostered by the teacher. Cultural security refers to a learning atmosphere character-ized by learning exercises which are unique to groups of students from different racial or ethnic backgrounds.

Interpersonal security can be established in many ways. The threat of evaluation can be reduced by substituting forms other than that of the competitive examinations (shutting off a few alarm bells), by proposing communication goals such as those based on clarifying issues in the group which arise from doubts and questions by the students. In place of activities based solely on the memorization of grammar patterns and pronunciation drills, the teacher initiates activities based on human interaction or dis-course. The correction of errors is postponed so that the students are encouraged to speak freely. The teacher begins a series of time-limited group learning experiences, each with its reflection or self-evaluation period. The time limit contributes to security because the experience is placed in the framework of an agreement which is easy for the students to grasp. The students find the painful experience of speaking a foreign language less threatening if it is to last for ten minutes rather than for an undetermined time span. All these steps contribute to the smooth function-ing of the communicative clock because the activities are diverse enough to encourage the development of many linguistic skills.

Cultural security can be established by adopting learning exercises which are unique to the background of the learners. An example is self-introduction, which is characteristic in both Japanese and American cultures. In American culture, the self-introduction is a rather informal ritual to be got through as quickly as possible. The purpose is to spend more time on the goals of the group. In Japanese culture, self-introduction is a protracted and highly formalized ritual. Every detail about each participant is considered important. American teachers of Japanese groups would provide more security if self-introduction were handled more slowly and systematically. A group of teachers from England, on the other hand, were very anxious during a self-introduction exercise which was being held in a CLL group between Japanese and American members. According to their explanation, the person does not introduce himself or herself in

British culture, but is presented to the group by the introduction of another. Each culture has its unique forms which provide for acquaintance upon forming new groups. These must be carefully adapted so as to provide cultural security for the students of foreign language. By establishing interpersonal and cultural security, the teacher has plugged into the student clock and appealed for psychological rather than mere physical presence. Curran has described the effect as follows:

> As 'whole persons,' we seem to learn best in an atmosphere of personal security. Feeling secure, we are then freed to approach the learning situation with an attitude of willing openness. Both the learner's and the knower's level of security determines the psychological tone of the entire learning experience: it is the foundation on which the other elements of SARD are built (1976, 6).

5.2.2. Attention-aggression

Within the secure environment, the next task of the teacher is to engage the student's attention in the learning experience. According to Curran (1976, 7), learning takes place somewhere along a continuum from uniqueness to boredom; something too new is too strange for us to hold in memory. It can also be highly threatening. On the other hand, something too familiar can deteriorate into boredom before it can be adequately learned. The ideal learning experience set up by the teacher strikes an area of interest which is balanced between newness and boredom. Values clarification exercises are an example of the kind of activity that can compel student attention within a secure classroom environment (question six). While receiving support from their fellow students as well as the teacher, students can talk about feelings and experiences that are important to them. Many such exercises can be found in Moskowitz (1978), Hawley & Hawley (1975), and Simon, Howe & Kirschenbaum (1972/1978).

5.2.3. Problems

The problem of the semester clock was how to build a supportive classroom community in a competitive situation (question four). In the CLL class, different kinds of large, small, and pair group experiences help build a community of students. The teacher's role is to outline the purpose of the learning experience and to set the time limits. The students are then free to take the initiative to act. This initiative has been called "Learner-Aggression" by Curran and has been toned down to "Assertion" by Stevick (1980, 111). Either of these terms is appropriate to characterize the attack on the problems of learning displayed by the students. Even though the teacher may need to remind the students of the necessity of mutual support in learning instead of the urge to defeat one another or merely to display knowledge, the students still possess the freedom to assert their efforts toward the learning goal.

The problem posed by the communicative clock was the need for the ability to shift linguistic styles with each new social environment (question five). The different social structures of the CLL class afford the student an opportunity to adopt a different style in a natural way. The teacher can facilitate shifts in social environment through his participation in large group activities and his absence from small group activities when students are functioning by themselves. The speaking style of the students shifts naturally from the formal style used in the presence of the teacher to an informal or intimate way of speaking when the students are conversing among themselves (cf. Joos, 1967, 11).

The flexibility of the CLL contracts allows for the use of time in either monochromatic or polychromatic ways (question two). According to the needs of the students, the teacher may implement a monochromatic time schedule with the whole class engaged in a single learning activity. The goals are focused rather narrowly on a restricted scope of foreign language skills. The demonstration of correct pronunciation skills may be held for the whole class, for example. The teacher may employ a polychromatic time schedule with the class divided into smaller groups, each with a different type of learning activity. The goals may be loosely fixed allowing each student the freedom to pursue personal goals. Both kinds of time schedule are necessary if we hope for gradual development in foreign language.

The communicative clock now begins to tick in harmony with the semester and cultural clocks. So far, five clocks have been synchronized: the teacher clock, the student clock, the cultural clock, the semester clock and the communicative clock. The teacher and the student clocks were harmonized by listening and waiting on the part of the teacher. Supportive group activities left the students some scope for action. Alarms on the teacher and the semester clock were toned down and the emphasis was placed on a supportive cultural atmosphere in the classroom where communication could occur. As a result, the communicative clock became unstuck and began to function.

5.2.4. Reflection-Retention

According to Curran (1976, 8), retention is the final process of absorbing what is studied into one's self and being able to retrieve and use it later with ease. Retention is supported by reflection, especially if the reflection occurs in the foreign language. The CLL reflection period consists of two parts: a period of silence and a time for mutual reporting. During the silent portion, the individual is asked to reflect upon his performance during the group learning experience. During the time for mutual reporting, the individual is asked to express, in English, his thoughts about his performance. The period of silence cannot be underestimated for its impact on learning. The silence helps the individual to focus on the learning forces of the past hour, to assess his present stage of development, and to re-evaluate future goals. The developmental clock, which spans the three time dimensions, past, present and future, is activated by the student himself as he consults with himself about his needs and goals in relation to the events of the class (question seven). The time components of learning can be clearly seen in the following example of student reflection: "Today, I spoke a little. I have not yet overcome my anxiety in speaking in the large group, but I am going to keep trying."

During the reflection period, the teacher helps the students to become free from the negative affects, doubts, and difficulties which impede learning. The teacher's clarification, through counseling responses of what the student is trying to say, supports the development of the student as a person as well as a second language speaker. Whole-person development occurs when the student can clearly see his own progress or areas of deficiency. In planning subsequent class activities, the teacher can tune himself with greater precision to the needs of the students by taking into account the feedback in the reflection periods.

5.2.5. Discrimination

When the students have retained a body of material, they are ready to sort it out and see how one thing relates to another. This discrimination, as the SARD mechanism repeats itself, becomes progressively more refined and enables the students to use the language for purposes of communication outside the classroom. Many Japanese speakers of English shy away from communicating in English with foreigners. In contrast, the members of a CLL group are likely to become motivated to establish speaking relationships with foreigners outside the classroom, because they are using the language for communication in the classroom rather than memorizing a set of pattern drills. Though non-CLL classes might have the same effect, the difference occurs later in the unifying effect in-class reports of such attempts have on the group. Reports of success encourage other members of the class to try out their English. This encouragement, along with diverse classroom experiences, helps the students apply their knowledge to new social encounters outside. The barrier between the real world and the classroom begins to diminish and the social clock constitutes a positive reinforcement for classroom learning rather than an obstacle (question three).

5.3.0. Summary

The purpose of this chapter was to explore the hidden and unstated messages of time which influence the progress of classroom learning, to look at the problems these messages cause, and to discover solutions to these problems through CLL. The clock analogy, as presented by Joos (1967), was used to state five principles concerning first language use. As accommodated and applied to second language acquisition, the five principles can help us to understand the implicit messages of time being sent to students in our classrooms. The cultural clock, the social clock, and the semester clock stem from the context of the historical age and time limitations under which we work. The communicative clock, the student clock, the developmental clock, and the teacher clock are more subject to our control. The clocks are in disarray and present eight questions which must be resolved if we are to hope for effective teaching—learning.

The last two principles of Joos were applied in Part 2. The teacher uses a series of "commitment mechanisms" (Kanter, 1972) called SARD (a cryptonym for six elements of CLL, namely, Security, Attention-Aggression, Reflection-Retention, and Discrimination). The eight questions of Part 1 were answered in the framework of SARD, a time learning system which is focused on the personal development of the participants. When all the clocks are ticking in harmony, the result is a consistent appeal for dedication to the difficult task of teaching and learning a foreign language.

Chapter 6
Social and Cultural Silence

6.0.

The focus of this chapter is upon silence as a psychodynamic as well as cultural phenomenon. According to Stevick (1976b, 119), the Greek term "psychodynamics" translated into Latin would be something like "intra- and interpersonal action," and in plain Anglo-Saxon, "what goes on inside and between folks." Social silence in the interpersonal dynamics of CLL refers to silence on the part of the teacher, the students, or when called for by the CLL contract, for example, during CLL reflection periods. As a cultural phenomenon, silence is a creative response occurring in a specific cultural context with attendant attitudes, codes of conduct, and values toward silence and speaking fully operative. For whatever reason, silence may occur in our foreign language classrooms, but its significance and importance for progress in speaking ability may go ignored or unattended. The purpose of Part 1 is to show how teachers can use social silence to promote progress in foreign language, even if they do not employ CLL. Part 2 describes five typical Japanese attitudes toward speaking and silence. In Part 3, learning contracts which challenge the negative aspects of silence are considered.

PART 1: SOCIAL SILENCE

6.1.0. Social Silence

Social silence triggers affective reactions which can foster or destroy the teaching relationship. Curran (1972, 112) has noted that teachers must recognize that the very process of presenting an idea may produce an "affective bind" for one or more of the students. This can happen in- advertently even in the CLL classroom, but the harmful effects of social silence can be neutralized during a reflection or evaluation, which is part

71

of the CLL learning contract. In the following discussion, we will identify some of the affective binds triggered by social silence through three types of CLL group conversation experience. Secondly, the uses of social silence will be shown in both CLL experience and reflection sessions.

6.1.1. Affective Binds in Three Kinds of Group Conversation Experience

(a) Type I. Type I experiences are held in large groups, or even with the whole class, as described in Chapter 3.1.4. During a Type I experience, the silent presence of the teacher places a demand for activity on the students. At the same time, such a silent demand provokes anxiety because the students are not sure how to respond or what to expect from the teacher if they are courageous enough to break the silence. Japanese groups often force individuals who are more proficient to speak as group representatives. Unpleasant anxiety expressed through long periods of silence frequently occurs during a Type I experience. If the anxiety is not properly handled by the teacher, the resulting silence will destroy the English-speaking experience.

(b) Type II. In a Type II experience the class is divided into small groups of five or six students who converse among themselves for a limited time period. The teacher is totally silent, allowing the English learning to occur among the students themselves. He stands ready to assist the students if they request his help. The basic task of the Type II activity centers upon the establishment of an English-speaking identity. Brown (1973, 233–4) has described the task as follows:

> Even in cases of 'instrumentally' motivated language learning, a person is forced to take on a new identity if he is to become competent in a second language. The very definition of communication implies a process of revealing one's self to another. Breakdowns in communication often result from a person's unwillingness to be 'honest' in revealing this self. A strong language ego is thus conceivably positively correlated with success in second language learning.

With his own meager resources, the individual student is left in a bind over the accomplishment of the task. The students as a whole may cling unduly to the security of their small groups and ask for a repetition of the activity for a number of classes. In effect, they prematurely declare independence from the teacher. Less motivated students are prone to use the native language during the small group activity. Though the teacher is available, few students consult with him. Consequently, a second bind arises from the silence of the teacher. If the silence is overly prolonged, the small group activity gradually degenerates into a class picnic (as one student described it) without any learning. Ultimately, the students have to choose whether or not to allow the teacher to contribute his knowledge to the group. The affective bind involves the willingness of the students to sacrifice some of their independence in order to give the teacher some scope for action.

(c) Type III. In ordinary classrooms, especially if the number of students is large, the teacher loses contact with the whole group in dealing with individuals. This introduces ambiguity into the interpersonal dynamics of the class. One result, among others, is a rapid increase in anxiety which cannot be tolerated for long by either the students or the teacher. In a CLL class, a Type III experience occurs when the teacher is partially silent. He is silent to the whole group, but active and participating in English conversation with individuals. It is the supportive CLL group contract that resolves the ambiguity in the interpersonal dynamics of the class. By agreement, each student is given the same chance to meet with the teacher. The whole class, including the teacher, is divided into pairs for brief, time-limited periods of English conversation. Each class member and the teacher receive a new conversation partner every three minutes. Even in a large class, a Type III experience can be prolonged for as long as forty-five minutes with great profit. The affective bind involves the willingness of the student to accept the responsibility for a one-to-one speaking relationship with the teacher and with each of his peers.

6.1.2. Uses of Social Silence

In the following sections, uses of social silence will be discussed in connection with the reflection period after each of the three experiences described above. In order to show how social silence leads to growth in language learning through the CLL stages, it will be necessary to refer once again to the types of experience. Therefore, this section will first discuss the reflection period after a Type I experience; second, the reflection period after a Type II experience; third, social silence and role reversal in a Type I experience.

6.1.3. Reflection after a Type I Experience

After the student has been given time to formulate his reflections of a Type I experience, some reference to the silence occurs in almost every report. If the student can not give the reason for his silence, the teacher should ask: "Why were you silent?" The reply touches the basic motivation of the student and his performance during the experience: "I was silent because I was afraid." Through the use of social silence, the teacher is able to assist the student to identify basic deficiencies in motivation. Sharing the experience of fear is often sufficient to dissipate its harmful effects. The teacher can both point to problems and suggest concrete remedies. For example, the silence can be broken very quickly with a simple question to someone in the group. Japanese students are surprised to find that it is not necessary to say something deep in a foreign language. In order to overcome fear, courage and struggle are necessary for the difficult task of mastering a foreign language. The responsibility for the content of the conversation lies with the whole group, not with individuals who are forced to speak by group pressure. Fear and silence should be made objects of a common struggle, and the students should be urged to help each other to overcome obstacles in the way of communication. These suggestions prove very helpful to students who find themselves struggling with the anxiety of Stage I.

6.1.4. Reflection after a Type II Experience

Reports after a Type II experience show that contact with the teacher has not been lost completely. Students in Stage II come to realize that they repeat the same grammatical mistakes again and again in their small groups with no one to correct them. Separated from the teacher it is difficult to learn and retain new expressions. Even less-motivated students find the honesty to express the need for the presence of the teacher to stimulate conversation in English rather than in Japanese. These comments show that the students have succeeded in establishing a basic identity, in the sense discussed in Chapter 3, as speakers of English. After a series of Type II experiences, students realize by way of honest reflection, that some contact with the teacher has to be re-established even at some cost in effort. The way is now open for a solution of the adolescent crisis of independence (Stage III). Now the teacher can intervene in the learner space without breaking the integrity of the group, a difficulty met by Berwick (1975, 288).

6.1.5. Social Silence and Role Reversal

After several sessions of small group activity and reflection, a return to Type I experience meets a different reception. By this time, the students have overcome their initial anxiety and are ready to provide an understanding atmosphere for the helpful role of the teacher. They are willing to share the learner space with the teacher. While the students, having passed from Stage III to Stage IV, are developing the subject of a conversation, the teacher finds himself active as coach and cheer leader of the lively action. The silence has vanished. While the students are struggling along totally in English (though semigrammatical), the teacher begins to give instructions about correct English. It becomes possible to publicly correct the mistakes of the students without disturbing the flow of the conversation. In my experience, at this point I have given grammatical directions almost totally in Japanese. The students in Stage IV have adopted a total English-speaking role, whereas their teacher is active in a Japanese-speaking role. The role conflict of Stage IV has been resolved through the switch. The threat of annihilation (Curran, 1972, 92) simply does not occur because the teacher is being used by the groups as a resource person. Seemingly, the dynamic silence of the teacher in his English-speaking role constituted an encouragement for the adoption of their English-speaking role by the students.

6.1.6. Reflection after a Type III Experience

Students in Stage V have achieved fluency and ability to handle a foreign language. Theoretically, they are able to accept the challenge of a one-to-one speaking relationship with their teacher (in the present case of a native speaker) and their peers. How are their achievements to be evaluated? In reflection, the teacher can still use partial silence to set criteria for the fulfillment of the contract. After a Type III experience, the reflection period is begun with a few appreciative remarks about the way individuals struggled to speak one hundred percent in English with the teacher himself. However, the purpose of the Type III experience is also for students to help each other achieve 100 percent usage in English. The teacher can ask the class to answer two questions: First, state in percentage the amount of English and the amount of Japanese which you used with your partner; second, did you give and receive support from your partner in speaking English? The teacher allows time (perhaps ten minutes) for the students to reflect and waits in silence. The reply to the first point, because of the restrictive nature of Japanese politeness, is speaking in terms of 30–40 percent English usage on first attempt. The teacher can reply to this by encouraging a higher percentage next time. Instead of scolding, the teacher has broken silence to set a higher goal for the student. In the interpersonal dynamics, the effect of the teacher's partial silence is a sharing of the responsibility for fulfilling the contract. In reply to the second question, the students in my experience have been able to form a greater number of positive English-speaking relationships in the CLL class than in classes based on other methods of teaching conversational English. These relationships were carried on in English even outside of class. The only difficulty with the Type III experience comes from the fatigue caused by the intensive English-speaking activity.

PART 2: CULTURAL SILENCE

6.2.0.

Cultural silence will be exemplified in five typical Japanese attitudes toward language. Each attitude contains an affective bind derived both from the native culture and from the language learning process. The challenge to the teacher involves dissolving these obstacles to learning. Only then can cultural silence be used to promote progress in English-speaking ability.

6.2.1. Five Typical Japanese Attitudes toward Language

Five typical attitudes of the Japanese towards verbalization and silence have been described by Masao Kunihiro (1974a; 1974b; 1976). The teacher of foreign languages will invariably meet these attitudes in one form or another when dealing with Japanese learners. Cultural silence is like a double-edged sword. If not handled properly by the teacher, it may give rise to affective reactions which hinder progress, and may eventually destroy the teaching relationship. Cultural silence, if correctly employed, can greatly reinforce and strengthen the impact of the learning experiences on the students. Each cultural attitude will be explained in a double way, both as an affective bind which hinders progress and as a challenge to the teacher of foreign language. The challenge consists of a creative task which must be accomplished if we are to hope for progress in foreign language acquisition. The five attitudes will be discussed under the following headings: first, the aesthetics of silence; second, alienation and identification; third, lack of confidence in contracts; fourth, lack of confidence in language; fifth, the problem of leadership.

6.2.2. The Aesthetics of Silence

A cluster of attitudes called "the aesthetics of silence" makes a virtue out of reticence and a vulgarity of verbalization or open expression of one's inner thoughts. This attitude can be traced to the Zen Buddhist idea that man is capable of arriving at the highest level of contemplative being only when he makes no attempt at verbalizations and discounts oral expression as the height of superficiality (Kunihiro, 1974b, 13 and 14). This attitude presents difficulties enough for the teacher of conversation, but it is even reinforced by a taboo of speaking out of place before a person who is higher in the social hierarchy (Kunihiro, 1974b, 12). For example, Japanese are usually reticent and anxious in the presence of a teacher or a native speaker of English. If the teacher is unaware or disrespectful of this attitude, Japanese students may resist his efforts to establish group discussion in the class. The creative task for the teacher is to present learning experiences through which Japanese speakers can learn to handle their anxiety and speak English in the presence of a teacher or native speaker of English.

6.2.3. Alienation and Identification

Japanese attitudes toward language are connected with problems of alienation and identification with one's peer group. Japanese groups look for complete consensus of feeling before taking a course of action. It is difficult for them to act with one segment of the group disagreeing (Kunihiro, 1974b, 8). Expressing one's own inner thoughts is restrained not only to avoid hurt feelings but also from the strong fear that by opening one's heart with full candor, one might become isolated from the group to which one belongs. Kunihiro (1974a, 20) has written:

> Here in Japan on the whole, meaningful communication or oral communication in particular is restricted to one's in-group; family, close friends or high school chums . . . It is extremely difficult for the fresh entrant into a company to engage himself in a free *tête-à-tête* with the president of his corporation, for example. If we use the term 'in-group' rather extensively, we can say that meaningful communication is restricted more or less to one's in-group.

The second task of the teacher, therefore, is to present a variety of learning experiences which allow interaction in peer groups. Interaction in such small groups will provide the students a chance to identify with English as a language of personal communication with others.

6.2.4. Lack of Confidence in Contracts

Contempt for language can also be seen in the attitude of even the most progressive companies toward contracts (Kunihiro, 1974b, 11). It is still quite common to have unwritten contracts between large manufacturers and trading firms; often, contracts seem to exist only for the purpose of specifying stipulations that are exceptions to the rule. Contracts often contain escape clauses which allow further negotiations as the basis for relationships between companies. "The contract is just a lot of words," according to Kunihiro (1974b, 15), "the reality exists somewhere apart from it." Japanese attitudes toward contracts will affect the learning contract between the student and the teacher in the classroom. If Japanese students are not given a chance to review the learning contract, the teacher may be faced with increasing resistance to learning from the students. The third task of the teacher is to establish confidence in a learning contract as the basis of acquiring ability in foreign language.

6.2.5. Lack of Confidence in Language

Japanese place comparatively light emphasis on overt linguistic expression (Kunihiro, 1976, 270). The foreign teacher who expects to base his conversation class on lively clash of ideas in debate may be in for trouble. Language in Japan has only been a way of casually throwing the other guy a ball in order to get a reaction from him on which to base one's next action (Kunihiro, 1974b, 11). Therefore, the fourth task of the teacher is to establish confidence in language as a vehicle of communicating ideas. Kunihiro (1974a, 22) has strongly emphasized this point as follows:

> I think that it is indispensable that at the very outset you should try to regain, restore, create, or generate, no matter how you put it, confidence in language as a vehicle for communication and this is particularly important in our case because we traditionally have not held language in very high esteem.

> This may sound a bit sermonizing but this realization is the most important ingredient in any formal or informal training program in the attainment of a better command of any language, particularly of any western language, English included.

> I would like to pointedly emphasize the importance of this psychological tuning, for want of a better term, to the utility of language as a vehicle for communication.

6.2.6. The Problem of Leadership

The leader in Japanese society tends to be a silent person. He fosters the group discussions from which decisions emerge. This attitude may present difficulties to a teacher who expects to develop leadership in his conversation class. The American leader tends to be more articulate. That is, he presents creative and original ideas he hopes the group will accept. But one qualification for being a "big shot" in Japan is silence — to say very little and with complete lack of eloquence (Kunihiro, 1976, 272). Those who consider their positions worthy of respect, scorn verbal argument as silly, an indulgence for immature school boys. Such a person leaves verbal communication to his subordinates, muttering only a significant word or two at the appropriate time (Kunihiro, 1974b, 15). The fifth task of the teacher is to exploit the cultural attitude toward silence. In the course of communicating knowledge of English, the teacher should be willing to change from an active participant to a silent role at many levels of the group interaction. This is a learning task for the teacher. He should learn to use cultural silence itself for the development of leadership among his students.

PART 3: USES OF CULTURAL SILENCE IN THE INTERPERSONAL DYNAMICS OF CLL

6.3.0. CLL Contracts

The purpose of this section is to show how the five tasks described above are carried out in a CLL community. In the previous descriptions of CLL, we saw that CLL is a learning contract which consists of both group experience and reflection. In this section, we will describe learning contracts which are tailored to meet the needs of Japanese students at the different CLL stages. The contracts are dynamic in the sense that changes occur in the role of the teacher, among the students at different stages of CLL learning, and in the contracts themselves. For instance, at Stage I and Stage IV, the contracts are the same but the reactions of the students are different. Because the needs of the students are similar, contracts at Stages II and III are treated together. The role of the teacher changes as he operates on different interpersonal dimensions of the CLL community. Some of the contracts call for an active teacher; others call for a more silent role for the teacher.

6.3.1. A Contract at Stage I

A contract at Stage I consists of the experience of silence and its reflection period. Because of the high value placed on silence, Japanese are not unaccustomed to membership in a group of silent people. To begin a course in English conversation from a base of silence is in accord with

Japanese cultural traditions. There are two ways of doing this. One way is to introduce the class as a short-term counseling session (Curran, 1972, 5). This can be done very easily in the first class of the semester. The teacher enters the class and remains perfectly silent until the first reaction comes from the students. The period of awkward silence lasts for five, ten, or, in some cases, longer than twenty minutes. The reaction is highly unpredictable. Sometimes the following questions occur. "When are you going to begin the class?" or "Why don't you start?" Sometimes the reaction takes the form: "I don't understand the meaning of this silence." On one occasion the following reaction occurred after thirty seconds of silence: "I was in your class last year and I know we are supposed to speak English." After the first reaction, the teacher makes his initial explanation of the basic contract with its time limits, educational requirements, the purpose of the class, the kinds of speaking experiences, and so on. Another way to begin the first class is to arrange the students in pairs and have them sit in silence for a moment or two before beginning with self-introduction.

6.3.2. Reflection after the Experience of Silence

The experience of silence is characterized by both anxiety and long periods when none or only a few students speak English. During the reflection period afterwards, reference to the unpleasant silence occurs in almost every report of the students. The reason for the silence relates to the basic motivation of the student and his performance during the experience period as we have seen previously (6.1.3.).

6.3.3. Contracts at Stages II and III: Small Peer Groups (Nakama)

The experience of silence is painful, but necessary for students. The teacher can reduce the pain by temporarily withdrawing from the class activity in silence. He can permit the learning to occur among the students in small peer groups called "Nakama." At Stage II, the class can be divided into groups of five or six students for a CLL exercise called the "Paper Drama." Each small group is given the task of composing and presenting a Japanese paper drama in English. The themes are decided by the group and are composed in English. Then the students are given the art materials which they need for the production of their drama. When finished, they are presented to the whole class with dialogue in English, music, the use of puppets, and drums. A more detailed description of the Paper Drama will be presented in Chapter 9 (9.1.6.).

6.3.4. Reflection after Peer Group Activity

Reflection after the peer group activity revealed that the students were aware of their distance from the teacher. They all attempted to reduce the distance by expressing the wish for closer participation with the teacher. On their own initiative they began to employ the skills of the teacher in correcting mistakes, stimulating communication in English, and asking for his constructive suggestions during the Paper Drama project. The realizations gained through reflection helped the students to gain confidence in the learning contract with the teacher as a means of learning English.

6.3.5. Cultural Silence and Role Reversal

In Stage III the students showed much more confidence in accepting foreign language speaking. First, silence was replaced completely by lively, active conversation, even though the English was semigrammatical. Secondly, the responsibility for developing the topic of a conversation was accepted by the students. Thirdly, as a teacher I found myself giving the explanations and directions necessary for speaking correct English in Japanese. The role conflict of Stage IV was resolved through the switch. Seemingly, the silence of the native speaker in his English-speaking role encouraged the Japanese students to adopt the English-speaking role. The dynamic role silence also had the added effect of communicating confidence in English as a means of exchanging ideas among Japanese themselves. If so, then cultural silence greatly contributed to the accomplishment of task number four, the establishment of confidence in English as a vehicle of communication.

6.3.6. A Stage V Contract

English conversation between a native-speaking teacher and each individual in the class is extremely difficult to establish, especially if the class is large. When the teacher begins to deal with individuals, he loses contact with the whole group. This introduces ambiguity into the interpersonal dynamics of the class. One result, among others, is a rapid increase in anxiety which can not be tolerated for long either by the students or by the teacher. As a former student of judo I stumbled quite by accident upon a way of solving this problem. In the Japanese judo hall, members are paired off in two long lines for feinting practice (Uchikomi) or a brief wrestling session (Randori). The point of each encounter is to become stronger in a single tactic or to grapple with a strong opponent for a short time (three minutes). In this way, the strong become stronger and the weak members are not overwhelmed. The face-to-face group can be introduced in the same way. The whole class is divided into pairs for short English conversations. Each member of the class and the teacher receive a new conversation partner every three minutes. After discovering that this type of activity was effective in establishing English-speaking relationships, I examined the Kendo and Karate clubs. Their basic learning patterns were the same as I had seen in the judo hall. Obviously, I had accidentally stumbled upon a culture-learning pattern that was adaptable to the English class. This was how the Type III experience was discovered.

6.3.7. Summary

The purpose of this chapter has been to show how silence influences learning progress. Social silence refers to the teacher's silence. Cultural silence consists of the attitudes, codes of conduct, and values toward silence and speaking with respect to a specific group of learners. The purpose of Part 1 was to show how teachers could use social silence to promote progress in foreign language even if CLL is not employed. Part 2 described five typical Japanese attitudes toward speaking and silence. Contracts which challenge the negative aspects of silence were briefly considered in Part 3. Further references to CLL contracts are made in Chapters 3 and 11. For whatever reason, silence seems to occur in learning contexts inside and outside the classroom, but its significance and importance for progress in speaking ability may go ignored or unattended. This book makes frequent reference to another dimension of silence called reflection. The importance of silence and group reflection in learning can not be overestimated. In the next chapter, the focus is upon a pattern of individual reflection and its impact on learning progress.

Chapter 7

Reflection in the Context of Community Language Learning

7.0

Current theories of learning have stressed experience as the basic context in which a second language is acquired. Recent examples are to be found in Dakin (1973). However, CLL, while not denying the importance of experience, has the unique quality of also employing reflection as a way of learning a foreign language. The purpose of this chapter is to show how the discipline of reflection contributes to language learning. A pattern of reflection will be demonstrated, and the importance of reflection as a teaching method will be considered. By introducing a period of reflection, foreign-language teachers might improve the effectiveness of their class activities without changing the methodology which they currently employ.

PART 1: A PATTERN OF REFLECTION

7.1.0.

During the course of using CLL in my oral English classes for nearly ten years, the students' comments resulting from a reflection period have followed a pattern. The purpose of this section is to describe the pattern that was observed. The effects of reflection on the learning progress of the individual and the group will also be pointed out. The pattern of reflection consists of the following five steps: (a) a statement of performance; (b) an evaluation of the performance; (c) a resolution for future performance; (d) comments upon the group performance; (e) suggestions for future class activities. Characteristic of the pattern forming the discipline of reflection is a widening of the individual and group awareness of the context of the CLL experience. This would have been lost without a reflection period.

7.1.1. Statement of Performance

At the beginning of his report, the student merely states what he did during the CLL experience: "Today, I was silent;" "Today, I was very active in class." The reasons for the performance are also given: "My cat died this morning, so I felt bad and couldn't say much." At this point, the teacher can react with a sympathetic remark or a kindly invitation to tell the class about the trouble. The sympathetic remarks of the teacher bind the cognitive experience of learning English with the affective state of the student at the moment. Such an experience in reflection may never be forgotten.

7.1.2. Evaluation of Performance

The student strictly evaluates his performance. He reports as follows: "Today, I did not speak at all because I was afraid. That is not good for my English." The teacher can express his frustration as follows: "You didn't speak. The time has passed and is lost. I can't bring it back." When the student realizes that he himself is responsible for the loss of his chance to advance in English, the effect is considerable.

Students quickly learn to compare the day's experience with that of previous classes: "Last week, I was too afraid to speak, but today I struggled hard to say something. Now I feel good for the effort." The teacher should try to find wide support in the class for such effort. Reports of success contribute much to the morale of the class. Evaluations of the performance of other students also contribute to the atmosphere, for example: "Today after Mr. . . . introduced an interesting topic, I was able to say something. Before that, I did not know what to say. I am very grateful because he helped me to speak."

Evaluation can also be built into the reflection period. Besides the general question about the class, the teacher may ask for an account of the students' performance. This is especially effective in the case of small-group activity in which the teacher has not participated. A second question can be put in the following form: "Please state, in terms of percentage, the amount of English and the amount of Japanese you used today." To anyone who reached 20 or 30 per cent of English, my reply would be encouraging: "That's very good. Why don't you try to raise your percentage next time?" In this way, the teacher gives the student a goal to work toward. In subsequent performance, the general average of the class might rise from 30 per cent to 60 or 70 per cent. Some individuals eventually achieve 100 per cent. From the point of view of evaluation, Begin (1971, 119) has written of CLL as follows:

> The importance of the evaluation session can hardly be over-emphasized. Man is not a mere mechanism of absorbing information; he is essentially an appraiser.

7.1.3. Resolution for Future Performance

The third step in the reflection process is a resolution for future perform-ance. The student's remark takes the following form: "Today, I was afraid, so I didn't speak at all. That is not good for my English. Next time, I am going to try harder." Such promises made by the individual before the group are considered serious, for they involve commitment to a learning contract which is at the heart of CLL discipline. Subsequent classes usually show more active participation by the student. It is important to show the timid student that he is not alone in his struggle with fear. Many experience it and the struggle to overcome it must be undertaken as a common class project. Sharing the sense of fear during the reflection period is sufficient to dissipate or diminish its effects.

7.1.4. Comments about the Group Performance

The individual makes some comments about the performance of the whole group. It may appear as follows: "Many people arrived late for class, so it was difficult to start at once. We had better come on time for class." Remarks on the part of two or three students are sufficient to bring about a noticeable improvement in later classes. At this point, students are more prepared to accept reprimand from the teacher after the discipline of reflection. For instance, the teacher can chime in by "blowing off steam" in agreement with the previous comment, and add others of his own about the exasperating aspects of the class performance. Regarding the CLL discipline brought to the class by the students, Curran (1972, 22) has written:

The person of the learner is the source and center of the learning, and his commitment to the learning process is the manner by which he learns. The manner itself carries with it its own 'disciplina,' that is, its own necessary conditions of submission and self-control.

7.1.5. Suggestions for Class Activities

Given the CLL discipline, which is brought by the learner into the reflection period, what develops in the group over the period of a semester? First, through the suggestions for future class activities, individuals begin to grow into the learner space. However, in the Japanese case, the growth takes unique cultural forms. Social learning mechanisms characteristic of Japanese society become adaptive to English education through CLL. A typical example is the activity of self-introduction. The important point is that Japanese students will suggest such types of group activity for their English classes.

Secondly, anything contrary to the basic learning contract will be brought to notice, discussed, and remedied during the reflection period. An example is the use of Japanese. During reflection periods, the use of Japanese is necessary until the students are well on into CLL Stages III and IV. The students at Nanzan Junior College had a six-year background of English study, but no experience of the spoken English of a foreign teacher. Their cognitive knowledge of English could therefore be described as at Stage III or IV, whereas their affective and effective use of English was below Stage I. When the students had become used to speaking English independently through series of CLL exercises (to be described in Chapter 10), it became possible to ask the class to use English during the reflection period also. The response was in accord with the basic learning contract, though semi-intelligible English with many mistakes was in evidence at first. As the students continued to struggle for two months to make themselves understood during reflection periods, the quality of the English showed a remarkable improvement. Students achieved flexibility in grammatical usage and made fewer mistakes. The group martialed its creative force in such a way that from the discipline of CLL reflection a new English-speaking experience was born. The result was that more English was spoken during the CLL reflection than during the CLL experience period.

PART 2: THE IMPORTANCE OF REFLECTION

7.2.1. Surface Learning vs. Learning in Depth

The effects of CLL reflection are important for two reasons: first, for English education in Japan; second, because CLL fills the necessary conditions for a semantic theory of language teaching and practice, as proposed by Silva (1975).

Recently, Harasawa (1974, 76) painted a very pessimistic picture of the English education scene in Japan, maintaining that the most serious obstacles lie in the character of the Japanese. He wrote:

> The Japanese people are unduly addicted to or intoxicated by their own language — so much so that neither English nor any other foreign language can ever succeed in invading their linguistic subconscious.

The conditions which have been outlined by Harasawa are certainly not inaccurate. His is a valid complaint, that foreign-language teaching has been conducted on the surface of the Japanese consciousness. Ordinary Japanese learners have never really been able to convince themselves of the reality of the true "livingness" of English (Harasawa, 1974, 74). However, in the context of CLL, one can adopt a more optimistic attitude toward the success of future foreign language teaching in Japan. Cultural learning mechanisms, such as Japanese reflection in the CLL context, present learning experiences which penetrate deep into the consciousness of the Japanese. The barrier between the classroom and real life falls as the students speak of their extracurricular activities and interests. The students claimed that what they learned in the CLL class was how to handle an English-speaking relationship. This, they felt, was important not only as an academic experience, but also as a lesson in living.

7.2.2. Eight Principles

Silva (1975, 342–5) has laid down eight principles which must underlie any attempt to base language-teaching practice on a semantic theory of language teaching. In general, the idea that language learning consists of merely repeating a series of drills aimed at learning patterns has been abandoned in the CLL approach. Meaningful communication, stressing the important content of the message, has been adopted in CLL, especially through reflection. Besides phonological and syntactic factors, the affective aspects of learning are dealt with during CLL reflection periods. Deeper than the level of meaning (semantic level) and affect, research has shown that the language learning process in the CLL context becomes centered on values which are learned in community (as was shown in Chapter 3).

7.3. Summary

A pattern of reflection has been described in this chapter. The importance of CLL for English education in Japan and elsewhere has been considered. My aim is not to change the teaching methodologies of other English teachers, but to suggest the introduction of a CLL reflection period into their classes. Perhaps others may also find an improved effect in their teaching activities by simply sharing the reactions of their students.

Chapter 8

Some Implications of Counseling-Learning for the Study of Culture

8.0. Cultural Implications of Counseling-Learning (CL)

CL contains some important implications for the study of culture. There are two reasons for this assertion. First, CL depends not only on the understanding and skill of the counselor, but also on the response of the clients. No matter how great the skill of the counselor in establishing a learning relationship based on a psychological contract, no matter how empathetic the understanding of the counselor might be in assisting the clients to isolate and clarify the problem, the best of counselors will fail if there is no creative response by the clients. Second, the creative response derives from the heart of communication, which is culture, or nearly so — as others have written (Hall, 1973, 28; Condon and Yousef, 1975, 4). Within the scope of this chapter, culture is defined as the creative response of the learners. Consequently, if time and effort are spent analyzing the response of the learners, cultural norms and values underlying the response will become clear. The creative response contains implications for the study of culture in at least five areas: silence, experience, meaning, feeling, and value. These five aspects of CL will be explained in Part 1. The group response can then be studied in a CL-based foreign-language learning pedagogy called CLL. In Part 2, the basic concepts of CLL will be explained with a view to the study of the creative facets of CL explained in Part 1. Culturally based learning norms, the response of the clients, can be adopted to foreign language learning. Then culturally based learning norms together with CLL can be used for more effective classroom learning. Examples will be presented in Part 3 and elsewhere in following chapters.

90

PART 1: FIVE CREATIVE ASPECTS OF COUNSELING

8.1.1. Silence

One of the criticisms of counseling is that long, inefficient and wasteful periods of silence occur frequently during the sessions. This criticism, according to Hughes (1970, 109), is based on the assumption that absolutely nothing is done during the period when the awkward silence occurs. Actually, the silent period, as any counselor knows, may be the most fruitful portion of the session. The participant is balancing the turn of the group discussion with his own experience, background and observations. When there is a period of silence, everyone is thinking, weighing possible solutions to the problem under consideration, perhaps making and rejecting possible decisions. Perhaps more creative thinking actually takes place at that time than during any other part of the discussion. The floor is open during the silent period. Because the group is waiting for the first one to speak, and because it could be any individual in the group, each is preparing a carefully thought out statement. This very freedom to speak, to be the one to resume the discussion, is self-enhancing to each group member. Possible statements are fashioned and refashioned, clarified and reclarified, even though they might remain unspoken. And though they go unvoiced, their very completeness increases the eventual chance for a core of agreement throughout the thinking of the group members. This core becomes the basis for mutual understanding that leads to effective results in counseling.

8.1.2. Experience

Rather than thinking of experience as something prior to the functioning of cognitive processes and as something to which the person is ideally open, it is more appropriate, according to Wexler (1974, 59), to view experience as created by the person who experiences. This is not a philosophical position that denies the existence of a world outside one's window or an inner world of memories or bodily sensations. Rather, it is a statement derived from work in psychology which suggests that our experience of these worlds is mediated by and is the result of complex processes of transforming information derived from them. Although it was once fashionable in psychology to think of the person as a passive system that receives stimuli, it is now more appropriate to think of the person as actively selecting, operating on, organizing, and transforming information in his environment. This change has largely been the result of work in the study of attention, perception, cognition, and information processing that has stressed the active and constructive nature of these processes. Experience is not something existing, but what is created by the functioning of cognitive processes.

8.1.3. Meaning

According to Wexler (1974, 65), the activity of creating meaning structures to organize information and structure a portion of the psychological field is what the client is doing in the therapy hour. Whether the client is talking about his exhilaration, his failures, or his aspirations, the client is engaged in a process of organizing information and structuring some portion of his life. The process of creating meaningful structures does not differ from the processing of information in more mundane situations in life. However, what does tend to make the therapy hour different from information processing in other situations is that the information being processed is often highly significant to the client and occupies a major portion of his psychological field. We may, in fact, regard much of what a client does in therapy as a concerted attempt to achieve change and reorganization in his life. There are two very basic tendencies which underlie this attempt: a need for organization and order in processing information and a need for new experience and change. Man need not be dependent on the external environment for change, but can create it for himself via his own processing of information. Through his ability to create meaning, man has the potential to be his own source of reorganization and change. He can distinguish and synthesize new facets of meaning from the diverse and complex information he receives. An optimal style of client experiencing is heavily dependent on the use of this potential and consists of the activity of elaborating and organizing the ideal. Rarely do clients seem able to do this for themselves. That is why they come to therapy. Indeed, clients' problems may not be what they suppose, but rather the way in which the clients think *about* their problems. Clients' problems, according to Wexler (1974, 69), may be deficiencies in the way they process information. Their processing style is such that they are not able to process and organize information so as to create change and reorganization with respect to their problems.

8.1.4. Feeling

According to Butler (1974, 176), there are a great many varieties of feelings; some are suited to discursive (logically organized) language and some are not. Those that are, mainly have to do with coping with the world, with the milieu, the society, the group, and relationships. They have to do with impingement and encounter. At the opposite pole is the unsuitability of discursive thought and language for communicating much of that class of feelings which we designate as emotional. According to Butler (1974, 175), such feelings are not actually communicated or understood at all. They are rendered or depicted. Feelings, to be understood, must be objectified so that they exemplify the shape or the form of the feelings, with the result that feelings can be clearly perceived. When the counselor objectifies the feelings of the client many times, the feelings take on the character of information. The client comes to a kind of self-knowledge, symbolic, but not necessarily organized in a logical way. The knowledge of self encountered is akin in nature to the experience of painting, poetry, and music. Indeed, self-knowledge is just barely conceptualized discursively. It is the objectification or exemplification of feeling that is of paramount importance in the understanding of one's own or another's feelings.

8.1.5. Values

In addition to the process of taking or absorbing meaning and significance in experience, there is also the urge in the client to give, to invest, or reinvest in other persons and things. In giving, there is, first of all, the giving of himself. In a way different from knowing by taking into oneself, there is the investment of self, the giving of self in a complete way to what is somehow known. According to Curran (1969, 40), this is to go beyond knowing to loving. Among the many things and persons a man knows, he chooses some and makes a special commitment of his whole self in some way to them. This is experience, meaning, feeling, plus a degree of self-investment. Understandably then, such value-charged relationships often show themselves in both positive and negative emotions, arouse defences and even somatic disturbances. When a person cares for something or someone, he has invested his complete self, not simply his conscious awareness. Curran (1968, 27) has defined counseling and psychotherapy as follows:

> In this, then, counseling and psychotherapy provide us with a model for personal relationships, learning, and, in fact, for all situations where meaning and significance of what is represented have also to become personal values. When a person genuinely invests himself in these meanings, and is creatively involved with others in producing their adequate fruition, he has made them personal values. This bringing of meaning and representation into being so that they become values is the central process we see evident in counseling and psychotherapy. Such a model of both being and representing constitutes the conditions for authentic relationship and creative commitment to ourselves and others.

PART 2: COMMUNITY LANGUAGE LEARNING

8.2.0.

The purpose of Part 2 is to show how the counseling areas of Part 1 can be studied with CLL. These five areas of counseling have been isolated for special emphasis because the client's response is most creative here, and, therefore, growth and development occur here most often. Given the freedom of the counseling hour, the client's response is typical of the behavior of his group or society in these five areas. In this sense, counseling reflects culture. Consequently, the creative response of the learners in the foreign language context can be studied with CLL. CLL can be defined as a supportive language-learning contract which consists of group experience and reflection. Each part of this definition will be explained in relation to the five areas of Part 1, each of which then can become an object of specific research in the foreign-language learning context. First, supportive use of "Learner Space" (Curran 1972, 91) will be explained in relation to silence. Second, language learning in groups will be presented in connection with experience. Third, group reflection will be related to the search for meaning. Fourth, the solution of conflicts will be shown in relation to affects. Fifth, human development will be connected with the pursuit of values.

8.2.1. Silence: Learner Space

The CLL teacher contributes to creative thinking by his supportive silence and use of learner space. The constructive use of learner space can be seen in a short-term counseling session (Curran, 1972, 5). When the student or any other person approaches the teacher and asks for a few minutes conversation, no contract is made for the talk. Instead, the short time available, perhaps ten minutes or so, is taken advantage of without further delay.

8.2.2. Group Experience

CLL is group experience. In contrast to methods centered on individual study, CLL language learning takes place in groups. It is a manifest fact, too easily overlooked by educators, that man is born into and lives in social interdependence. His earliest, as well as recent, learning about himself and his world are set in the human context. An overwhelming proportion of cultural fantasy and impulse life (entertainments, arts, and literature) are concerned with the experience of living. If this focus is broadened to include all other forms of relationships, the preponderance is so massive as to be beyond comment. Man has evolved many forms of relationships: acquaintance, friend, intimate, companion, opponent, bystander; family, social group; cities and nations; lover, spouse; parent, and child; member, officer, outsider. Selecting, operating, organizing, and transforming his relationships in a creative way, man has discovered ways of relating with all degrees of intimacy, with varying amounts of formality, with wide-ranging or narrow substantive focus, with relatively complete or relatively restricted personal involvement, and so on. Through his experience, man forms alliances of many kinds, but except in quite recent times, meaningful ties have been those linking him with one other person (buddy, spouse), a small in-group (family, gang), and larger (but still quite limited) groupings which included other in-groups (village). It seems reasonable to suggest that this common and centuries-old human experience subtly permeates much of our thinking and feeling about relationships and doubtlessly affects our behavior, our language, and our learning. The three basic human experiences reported by Bugental (1965, 352) involve three relationship patterns: pairing, small groups, and large groups. The design for sensitivity training was called the "Dyads—Clans—Tribe Design." The design received an enthusiastic response from the participants because it seemed congruent with basic (primitive) human relationships patterns of living and learning. The Dyads—Clans—Tribe Design is very basic to CLL learning. Cultural experience can be studied in the pair, small and large group formations as was shown in Chapter 3. Additional examples in the Japanese case will be cited in Part 3.

8.2.3. Reflection: Exchanges of Meaning

The reflection period gives the group a chance to reorganize and restructure its information in such a way that both the operation of cognitive processes during the group learning experience and the object of those operations — the task itself — become clearer. The exchanges of meaning occurring during group reflection are more intense and more personal than the exchanges occurring during the group experience. The participants are reliving the experience in order to catch the facets of meaning which were only implied or overlooked during the stress of the group experience. Through reflection, group members create new learning experiences for themselves. The CLL reflective learning process is especially effective if group reflection itself is a function of the culture of the participants. Since not enough is known about the nature and effects of group reflection, this aspect of CLL provides ample scope for study of the exchange of meanings, an important facet of culture. Examples from Japanese culture will be cited in Part 3.

8.2.4. Affects: The Solution of Conflicts

CLL is learning. Curran (1972, 112) has shown that learning in the sense of exchange of meanings is not a neutral process. The very process of presenting an idea may place the learner in an affective bind. In CLL, the learner employs the medium of the target language to work out creative solutions. The characteristic style which the learner uses to process information and exchange meanings can be studied with CLL. Besides personal conflicts such as anxiety, identity, indignation, and so on (Chapter 4), the reconciliation of social and cultural differences can also be studied. Social conflicts derive from the needs of a learner to achieve a social position in his own culture. Social conflicts arise among junior college students, for example, around the need to obtain enough credits for graduation, to find suitable employment after graduation, and to settle down in marriage. The reconciliation of these needs and affects can be studied within the context of creative response. The students have suggested a drama exercise based on Japanese culture. Within the Japanese "Paper Drama" many of these social conflicts and their solutions find an objectified form.

8.2.5. Language Learning

CLL is language learning. Meaning, feeling and values are so interwoven in acquiring a second language that the three can be introduced as a single "Motivational Field." Curran (1969, 40) has written:

> This notion of value and the motivational field it implies, resulting as it often does in emotional states, might be expressed by the popular phrase 'vested interests.' 'Investing' signifies, of course, putting on clothes. In this sense, then, one has taken on 'interests;' that is, one has set up goals and achievements which one wants with some degree of intensity. This is creative tension. Emotions result from and are interwoven with such 'vested interests.'

Language learning is the development of people in the motivational field. The learner is given birth and grows in the new language, as has been shown in Chapter 4. The Japanese case with CLL exemplifies a specific form that growth takes.

PART 3: THE CREATIVE RESPONSE
OF THE LEARNERS

8.3.1. Silence

The purpose of Part 3 is to exemplify the CL/CLL norms presented in Parts 1 and 2. If we compare the response of Japanese, American and British groups to silence, the importance of learner space for the study of culture becomes clear. Given the learner space, all three groups were unanimous in demanding action and purpose during a demonstration of CLL for teachers of English. All three groups were uneasy and anxious about the initial silence of the CLL counselor. The response took different forms. The Japanese teachers were the first to suggest self-introduction because this is their norm on forming new groups. Self-introduction is repeated in a formal way each time a new group is formed for a specific purpose. The thought of self-introduction did not occur to a group of American participants. They resorted to a conversation about an imaginary voyage or trip, anything to dispel the increasingly high anxiety connected with the silence. They readily took up the suggestion of the Japanese teachers and began to introduce themselves. Self-introduction occurs only at first meeting in American society and, therefore, is held less frequently than in Japanese society. The British participants, on the other hand, were extremely anxious and increasingly disturbed by the self-introduction before the whole group. Such introductions in England are not handled by the individual himself but by another person, an acquaintance or good friend. The introduction by another is held on first meeting only, as in American culture, but in a more formal way. Here we have three different reactions to silence, each based on differing cultural norms. Therefore, we can conclude that the cultural norm probably dictates the reaction to silence. The same attitude is probably also connected with attitudes toward language, the subject of Chapter 6.

8.3.2. Experience: Culture-Learning Contracts

Learning takes place in social groups bounded by psychological contracts. As was shown in Chapter 3, these contracts take on indigenous forms called "Culture-Learning Mechanisms." In the Japanese case with CLL, culture learning reflects and exemplifies general social learning norms. Culture learning and culture-learning mechanisms, which are forms of creative-learning experiences, will be treated more extensively in Chapter 9.

8.3.3. Meaning-feeling

The construction of a paper drama is a small group activity which demonstrates "Objectification" in the reconciliation of personal, social, and cultural conflicts. The objectification consists of a story related by the learners to the counselor. The counselor replies in a cognitive way by correcting the English and improving the sequence of the story. The story is returned to the students and they retell it in an art form characteristic of Japanese culture. This is the "Paper Drama." As the narrator presents the story, a series of pictures depicting the action are presented. The effect of the dialogue is to make the pictures come alive. The theme of the story usually consists of some personal problem such as marriage, finding a job, the relationship with the teacher, or even a moral theme. The social theme consists of the solution of the problem by the characters themselves or by the intervention of a third party. Reconciliation of culture differences occurs in several ways. The story occurs in a Japanese setting with all the characters clothed in kimono, but the interaction takes place in standard American English. The story might also occur in a western or other foreign setting with all the characters in modern style dress. Even though the interaction occurs in standard American English, the style of address follows Japanese etiquette. There is a polite speech and the sequence of events occurs according to the ritual of a Japanese public ceremony. Another example of objectification of affects occurs during the "Interview," as will be shown in Chapter 10.

8.3.4. Values

There are two values which can be studied with CLL. First is a change of attitude toward language; second, an improvement in self-image. Study of the self-image of Japanese speakers of English (Chapter 11) will help us to understand how to promote improvement of self-image in the foreign-language learning context. Self-image and self-understanding form the basis for establishing a relationship with another person in the cultural context.

8.4. Summary

In the first part of this chapter, five areas of counseling were explained around the following elements of language: silence, experience, meaning, affect, and value. In Part 2, it was shown how the five areas of counseling could be studied with CLL. Part three was a brief exemplification of Parts 1 and 2 in the Japanese case.

Chapter 9
Culture Learning Mechanisms

9.0. Introduction

Japanese society provides a number of culture-learning mechanisms that are unique and interesting. Unique, because few other cultures, to my knowledge, possess the same traits; and interesting, because those mechanisms can be exploited to the fullest extent for the purpose of learning in general and second language acquisition in particular. Culture Learning mechanisms can be understood as types of group learning experiences, in the sense described by Egan (1970, 18), governed by a psychological contract. Culture Learning mechanisms are CLL contracts which are given specific dimensions in time and space. A group of people in the open situation of counseling will define the dimensions of their relationship according to the norms of their culture. These norms have been adopted by CLL and put to use for English education. Culture Learning mechanisms represent the group response to a given social situation. The local color given to the CLL contract is Japanese culture.

The task of this chapter is to describe, classify, and show how culture mechanisms work. The classification of culture mechanisms will be explained within the social dimensions of learning, as described in Chapter 3. Three of the more important ones, the age hierarchy, the Club-Gasshuku, and silence-reflection, will be described in Part 2. Exemplification by means of an experiment in a Japanese high school will demonstrate how they work out in a given setting. This will be done in Part 3.

PART 1: THE CLASSIFICATION OF CULTURE-LEARNING MECHANISMS

9.1.0. A Social Value-Model

Hirschmeier and Yui (1981, 44−52) have analyzed the historical development of Japanese business around a social value-model with four dimensions: vertical, horizontal, and depth (ie, time continuity). The fourth aspect, called "ethics of functional role expectation," was intended to clarify the strength of the unifying principle. The ethics of functional role expectation, according to Hirschmeier and Yui (1981, 52), consist of the external pressures generated by Japanese society on the individual to shape each man's thinking and doing to fit the generally expected social role in which he found himself. My Japanese acquaintances tell me that such external pressures are still characteristic of Japanese society today. In itself, the value-model of Hirschmeier and Yui has nothing to do with foreign-language education. However, I have observed that Japanese learners tend to define their relationships in terms of the value-model. Therefore, the model is helpful for an understanding of the reaction of Japanese students in our classrooms. The social dimensions are horizontal and vertical with respect to the teacher. Although the time continuity is much shorter than the periods of Japanese history which were analyzed by Hirschmeier and Yui, still, the continuity of the group life over a semester or a school year is a dynamic factor in the personal development of the participants and of the group itself. When a group operates on a psychological contract, the living community dispenses knowledge on both its horizontal and vertical dimensions. The ethics of functional role expectation in a Japanese CLL group operate especially through reflection, as was shown in Chapters 3 and 7, to insure optimal fulfillment of the contract by all the participants.

On the vertical dimension, learning occurs primarily between the teacher and the whole group; secondarily, between the teacher and each individual student in the group (Chapter 3). On the horizontal dimension, learning takes place among the students themselves. Furthermore, because learner space is provided by CLL, students are free, over the time continuity of a semester or school year, to construct group learning experiences patterned on their own cultural milieu. It is possible to classify the pertinent cultural mechanisms, in the Japanese case, within the social dimensions of the social-value model. On the primary vertical dimension are the culture mechanisms of the age-hierarchy and the club-workshop (Gasshuku). On the secondary level of the vertical dimension are the pair-group and the interview (Mensetsu). On the horizontal dimension are the self-introduction and the picture story (Kamishibai). The first two culture mechanisms were employed in an experiment to be described later in this chapter. The others were used inside the classroom as described in Chapter 3.

9.1.1. The Age-hierarchy

Examples of culture mechanisms on the primary vertical dimension of the social learning relationship are the age-hierarchy and the Japanese club with its workshop. According to Nakane (1970, 26), a hierarchy based on duration of service within the same group and on age rather than individual ability is overwhelmingly important in fixing the social order and measuring the social values of a Japanese group. Nakane has written (1979, 29):

> In Japan, once rank is established on the basis of seniority, it is applied to all circumstances, and to a great extent controls social life and individual activity.

CLL is also organized on a hierarchical basis. Curran's (1972, 128–35) five stages of growth form a learning hierarchy from the dependence of childhood to the complete proficiency of adulthood. The details of the CLL hierarchy and its effects on learning can be found in Chapter 4.

9.1.2. The Club-Workshop

The Japanese age hierarchy, for example, serves as the vertical social structure for an informal learning group called the "Club." The club is a unique Japanese social entity with no counterpart in an American school. The extracurricular activities of a modern Japanese school are organized into small, tightly knit social units of younger and older students. Clubs function throughout the entire school year on a hierarchical basis, the younger serving the older and learning from them. They operate on an allotment of funds from the students' association. Other than restrictions of a budget and the advice of their student counselor, the members are left to run their club as they see fit. Decisions concerning activities are made at the top of the hierarchy by the club captain and are then passed down the hierarchy where they are carried out by the various other officials in minor roles. Because of its security, Japanese students prefer to remain in the same club throughout their school days rather than change from one extracurricular activity to another. All the graduates of a particular school are identified by the year of graduation and membership in some school club.

9.1.3. The Pair-Group

The CLL social learning contract is enacted not only between the teacher and the whole group, but also between the teacher and each individual in the group. The secondary vertical dimension is between the teacher and each individual in the group, or a Type III experience (cf. Chapter 6). The idea for the Type III experience was originally derived from a Japanese culture-learning mechanism. In the Japanese judo hall, members form a double line for "Uchikomi" (feinting practice) and "Randori" (standing tactics). For feinting practice, each member chooses a single judo tactic and feigns an opening attack on his opponent for a fixed number of times. The number is counted off either between the pairs or by the whole group. Afterwards, all the partners are changed. For standing tactics, each member wrestles his opponent to the floor during a three minute period. Once the opponent is on the floor, that match is broken off and begins again from a standing position. One of the lines circulates so that each member receives a new opponent every three minutes. This is the way that judo is learned.

In the CLL class, the students are divided into two lines. They "wrestle" with an English conversation for three minutes (Randori). Partners are changed every three minutes. The teacher also enters the line and speaks with each student for a short time. However, because of time limitations, it is usually impossible to speak with each and every member of the class. The teacher has made a gesture (Uchikomi) which is interpreted by the students as a valid expression of interest in each member of the class.

9.1.4. The Interview (Mensetsu)

Another example of a cultural mechanism on the secondary vertical dimension between the teacher and the individual, is the interview (Mensetsu). If misunderstanding develops in a Japanese group, clarification of the social relationships can result by halting public activities temporarily. The whole group is divided into small units for an interview with the leader. Issues which are troubling either the leader or the members can be brought up and discussed in a private and secure manner. The application of the interview to foreign-language teaching—learning will be described in Chapter 10. The interview is so flexible that it can be used in many ways within or independently of CLL.

9.1.5. Self-introduction

Self-introduction on a horizontal level takes place frequently in Japanese society each time a new group is formed. Many other culture-learning mechanisms are connected with small group activity in which the teacher does not participate (Type II). Should it be required, the teacher stands by ready to give assistance. The students are allowed to exercise the foreign language which they have already learned.

9.1.6. The Picture Story (Kamishibai)

The picture story (Kamishibai) is a Japanese cultural form of story telling which can readily be adapted to a Type II experience. Each group is asked to compose a story in English. After the English to be used in the story has been corrected, the students depict the action on a series of about ten large picture cards. Once the dialogues have been matched to the pictures, each group presents its picture story to the whole class. American children would readily take to such a task, but a group of adults would consider it puerile. Japanese groups of all ages become deeply involved in the creative activities. The picture story is a valid form of Japanese culture-learning. The scenes depicted may be familiar Japanese scenes, but the people interact in standard American English. More often, the scenes consist of some realistic facet of American life. In either case, the psychological process is more than cognitive, or even affective. The cultural imagination of the students is engaged in color and form. The creative learning process of the picture story takes place on three levels, namely, the cognitive level (through the composition of the story in English), the affective level (by the creation of a plot which holds the interest and attention of the class), and on the imaginative level (by depicting the story in color and form).

During the class presentation, the stories can be videotaped. After each presentation, the teacher is expected to make his own comments and give his impressions of the story. The videotape can then be replayed to the class by way of review. The class presentation, itself derived from a Japanese culture mechanism, is called "Matsuri" (Temple festival). The gala occasion, or "Story Telling Festival" (Kamishibai Matsuri) can be made even more effective if it is accompanied by appropriate music. Students might not be willing to learn a page of dialogue from a text book, but they have no trouble comprehending the dialogues of a picture story.

PART 2: CULTURE-LEARNING MECHANISMS

9.2.1. The Age-hierarchy

The hierarchy system is observable in many sectors of Japanese society, one of them being education. Before the arrival of the modern school in Japan, the education of youth was carried on in small contractual groups around a single teacher (Dore, 1965). The contractual group, according to Egan (1970), operates on the basis of a series of rules that makes the group operative and gives it a sense of direction. The members agree, either explicitly or implicitly, to follow these rules in order to achieve the purposes of the group. The rules might change as the group moves forward, but at any stage in the development of the group, a set of rules is operative. This is the psychological contract which governs the group experience. Implicit in any psychological contract are the goals or purposes of the group and the means the group uses in order to achieve these goals. Contract groups are characterized by high "visibility," that is, the major features of the learning experience are clearly explained to the members before they subscribe to the contract. After they freely agree to join the group, they bind themselves to a common goal and strive to achieve it throughout the life of the group.

The learning contract in the ancient Japanese school was made between the pupil and the teacher (Dore, 1965, 72). Personal apprenticeship rather than institutional membership remained the dominant principle of organization (Dore, 1965, 73). The contract stipulated the amount of tuition and the learning conditions of the school. The learning contract was based on two assumptions: 1) learning took place in a disciplined social environment which involved the whole lifespace of the learner; 2) those who had achieved distinction in the learning hierarchy were expected to assume responsibility for the daily order of the school and for the education of those younger.

The hierarchy system, as a social mechanism in schools today, rigidly divides students into age groups and imposes an inflexible routine on teachers. In contrast, the routine of the ancient school was more flexible, but the rules were stricter. The youngest students under fifteen arrived at the school for an hour of instruction, not by the teacher, but by the boarders. Those who showed outstanding ability or interest in learning were allowed to reside with the teacher at the school. Only after an hour of class and after their young pupils had returned home did they eat breakfast. From about mid-morning they were joined by a group of day-students for their own formal learning. They were not confined to desks and lectured at for the whole day, but were allowed to ask questions and hold free discussion about their subjects. The teacher called on them individually or in small groups for formal sessions; otherwise, they were left free to read by themselves. Six times a month, they had classes in the modern sense of group reading in place of the free reading session. For this purpose, they were divided into three grades, those aged fifteen to seventeen, those aged eighteen to twenty, and those aged twenty-one and over. The age limits were not rigidly fixed, however, and bright students could reach the upper grades at an early age. In between, the system worked in such a way that the younger learned from older students, automatically, willingly, and appreciatively.

9.2.2. The Club-Gasshuku

One may observe the same hierarchical mechanism in the Club-Gasshuku, though in different form, operative in the social organization of the extracurricular activities of the modern Japanese school. Recreational activities are informal forms of learning that are carried on in focused contractual groups called "Clubs." According to Egan (1970, 61), contracts can be comprehensive, covering all facets of the group experience, or they can be focused, referring to specific facets of an experience. As comprehensive contractual units, extracurricular activities are organized into sports or cultural clubs. Among the cultural clubs, for instance, one can find small social groups focused on the narrow facets of activities, such as Western or Japanese chess.

Part of the cultural mechanism of the Japanese club is the annual or semiannual Gasshuku. The Japanese term *Gasshuku* can perhaps be equated to an English "Camp-in." However, the Gasshuku is in no sense as frivolous an affair as a camp-in. A camp-in, in the American sense, is usually a prolonged picnic for recreational purposes. The members of a camp-in usually desire a break from the routine, or the fleeting desire to commune with nature.

The workshop or Gasshuku is undertaken by each club as a serious social learning experience structured by a definite contract. The Gasshuku is usually undertaken as a group response to some ordeal such as a competition, or perhaps a group difficulty, for example, a decline in membership. The purpose of the Gasshuku is to prepare the whole person in mind, body, and emotions for the coming ordeal. The Gasshuku can be identified as a unique cultural mechanism by which the variously focused contracts are intensified in a living experience. Egan (1970, 76) describes five kinds of contracts or goals by which a group carries out its purpose; namely, contract, interaction, process, content, and need goals. Consideration of each of these goals together with two other cultural mechanisms will help us to understand how the Gasshuku operates as a social unit.

Meticulous planning goes into every detail of the contract goals, the major features of the Gasshuku experience. In a series of meetings held beforehand, the members decide the purpose, schedule, length, and budget of the Gasshuku. The schedule of activities, each of which Egan would consider a contract goal, is rigorously enforced.

9.2.3. Silence-Reflection

Besides the age-hierarchy system and the Club-Gasshuku, the cultural mechanisms of silence and reflection are operative in any Japanese social group today. In the case of the Gasshuku, silence and reflection are pursued with vigor. While the schedule of activities reflect the contract goals of the group, the interaction goals are seen in the kinds of side activities which are allowed or forbidden to a group in its free time periods of silence. Egan (1970, 76) says that interaction goals are necessary for the fulfillment of the contract and lie at the heart of the contract experience. During the Gasshuku, for example, free periods are not intended to be vacuous times of meaningless social activities. Intellectual or religious pursuits carried on in silence are encouraged. Silence during the Gasshuku is considered a vital preparation of the mind for the group ordeal. If rest and recuperation were needed in the case of a judo Gasshuku, these were allowed as interaction goals. In the dynamics of the Gasshuku, in so far as the interaction goal of rest was used as preparation for the next judo encounter, it was transformed into a contract goal, hence as something allowed. However, if rest occurred in the activity of the judo practice, it was interpreted as hindering the enactment of the contract. Consequently, it was forbidden and severely punished as we shall see.

Each evening during the Gasshuku, a period of group reflection is held for about an hour. Each activity of the day is reviewed in terms of content and process. Egan (1970, 77) says that content goals are the events of the schedule in the ideal, for example, in the plans made by the group before the Gasshuku. Process goals refer to the way in which a group carries out its activities. In the dynamics of the Gasshuku, the discrepancy between the ideal and the actual performance gives rise to a sense of corporate guilt, "existential guilt" according to Egan (1970, 215), which is expiated by a ritualistic system of rewards and punishments. Besides his prerogatives of command, the leader enjoys judicial authority to separate the heroes of the day from the villains in a brutally impartial way. Since he is the guardian of the contract, he also exercises power to condemn, punish and absolve from guilt.

Cultural mechanisms, such as the age-hierarchy, the Club-Gasshuku, and the custom of reflection and silence, among others, are still functional in the contemporary Japanese educational scene. Most modern methods of formal pedagogy are not culturally based on learning mechanisms operant in the indigenous society, but are cognitive forms which are often imported. Consequently, modern students are left with affective blocks of unfulfilled needs in learning, especially in regard to the mastery of foreign language. While counseling Japanese students who have cognitive learning difficulties in foreign language, affective and cultural variables had to be dealt with. Affective aspects of the learning process, called "need goals" by Egan (1970, 77), refer to the tendencies of individuals to use a group situation to fulfill personal needs. Brown (1973) also stressed consideration of affective factors or need goals in dealing with cognitive difficulties in language learning. Brown (1973, 231) writes:

Though all the optimal cognitive factors may be operating in the attempted solution of a given task, the learner may still fail because of an affective block.

Cultural mechanisms are valuable means, if coupled with a pertinent methodology, for removing affective blocks to learning. A form of learning close to their social milieu provides Japanese students a supportive learning experience in communication, rather than in competition and isolation from others. Furthermore, as has been shown, the three mechanisms are already functional outside the formal language learning instruction in the modern Japanese school. It is necessary to adopt these mechanisms for use inside the foreign language classroom. In dealing with learners as a social group, the three mechanisms of the age-hierarchy, the Club-Gasshuku, and silence and reflection can be seen as a unity, called "Culture Learning." These three learning mechanisms are found in almost every social institution in Japan. Therefore, it was easiest to deal with them as a single functional unit for the purpose of assisting Japanese students to fulfill their needs for a living social experience in learning.

PART 3: THE APPLICATION OF CULTURE LEARNING

9.3.0. An Extracurricular Experiment

The purpose of this section is to describe an experiment and the dynamics that occurred in the group as CLL was introduced in connection with the cultural mechanisms of Japanese society. The age-hierarchy, the Club-Gasshuku and silence-reflection were fully exploited in CLL as it was applied in the Japanese case. The setting was in the informal extracurricular activities of a school. Differences in age showed that, given the right cultural mechanism, CLL could be used with many different kinds of learning groups. The focus of group activity was the mastery of a foreign language, in this case, English.

9.3.1. Subjects

The experiment was set up in the English Speaking Society (ESS) of a Japanese high school. The subjects were twenty-five boys from Nanzan Junior and Senior High School in Nagoya. Age and English ability ranged from second year junior high school (age fourteen) to second year senior high school (age seventeen). Since they were willing to engage in ESS conversational groups even after a full day of classes and seven hours of English a week, the subjects could be described as well motivated. Activities in the ESS took place over a year during which the Gasshuku was held twice.

9.3.2. The ESS-club

CLL foreign-language learning occurred in the cultural context of the Japanese club, in the sense described previously. The club advisor, who functioned as a CLL counselor, assumed the role of a teacher in a traditional Japanese school. The ESS was a close-knit social unit in which the age hierarchy was fully operant. The older directed the younger in various foreign-language activities, such as free English conversations, outings in the country, the use of the telephone, and English letter writing. Since the Japanese age hierarchy provided a social structure for the club, the anxiety of the high school students, even in the presence of a foreign teacher, was not as overt as in the experiment described in Chapter 3. In fact, the hierarchical social structure of the Club-Gasshuku provided the experiment with its unique characteristics. Because of their youth, the cultural mechanisms of reflection and silence were not as overtly functional in the social dynamics of the ESS as in the experiment described in Chapter 3.

9.3.3. The ESS-Gasshuku

In its normal activities, a CLL discipline for learning was established in the ESS and gave the students a secure English speaking experience. However, once the CLL experience was intensified by the ordeal of the Gasshuku, the security of the group was disturbed by a crisis of responsibility in leadership that centered around the club president.

Rather than deprive the emerging leader of a chance to develop by taking over the details of the preparations, the club counselor shared the responsibility by engaging in a series of meetings during which decisions were made by the collective leadership at the top of the social hierarchy. They were left to be carried out by various members, by the president himself or by the officials of the ESS. The cognitive effect of the acceptance and fulfillment of responsibility by the president was an improvement in his foreign-language ability. This did not occur as an isolated incident or a mere cognitive phenomenon, but part of his total growth as an individual while he planned and executed his responsibility for the Gasshuku. Since the staff members did not know Japanese well, it was necessary for the president to discuss his problems, ideas, and requests in English. The whole person, his intelligence, emotions, values, and personal gifts, such as the power of persuasion, were all involved. As a result of the personal struggle to handle an English-speaking relationship, the student leader developed in all these areas, not only in mere cognitive ability in English. During the Gasshuku, the contract goals consisted of an intensive schedule of English language activities. As an interaction goal, the English-speaking rule was severely enforced. In fact, it became a norm of social conduct sanctioned by a ritualistic system of rewards and punishments. When the group norm was violated by a member who inadvertently spoke Japanese, a fine of ten yen was levied. The culprit had to bow three times before the punishment box that was decorated and displayed in a prominent place. The culprit was also required to apologize to the group for the violation. The further up the social hierarchy the violation occurred, the greater the enormity of guilt sensed by the members. Upon arrival at a Gasshuku for a visit, the author once witnessed a scene of great consternation and confusion. The club president, having just violated the English-speaking rule, was being carried bodily and summarily thrown on the floor before the punishment box to make expiation for his fault. Later, the money collected in the box was used to purchase small awards for the outstanding performance of those who participated in other English-speaking activities of the Gasshuku.

As process goals, the intensive English-learning discipline of the Gasshuku extended itself into the activities of the club (content goals) for the rest of the school year. During the Gasshuku, an English play and composition writing were on the schedule. The English play was rewritten and corrected, roles were assigned and practiced. Shakespeare's *Hamlet* was presented with great emphasis on the sword fight in the last scene during the annual school festival. The English compositions produced during the Gasshuku were gathered together and printed in the form of an ESS magazine at the end of the school year. The Club-Gasshuku filled a need for a different kind of learning from that of the classroom, namely, culture learning based on a group experience.

PART 4: RESULTS AND DISCUSSION

9.4.0.

The results of the experiment paralleled those of Chapter 3 in the follow-ing ways: a) progress in foreign language acquisition took place in a way that was significantly different from behavioristic learning; b) the learning atmosphere of CLL together with Japanese cultural mechanisms was conducive to second language acquisition; c) the anxiety characteristic of Japanese speakers can be handled in a supportive learning milieu; d) even silence can contribute to second language acquisition.

9.4.1. Culture Learning

First, progress in second language acquisition took place in a significantly different way from behavioristic learning. Far from being a mere repetition of foreign-language patterns, significant learning took place through the cultural mechanism of the Japanese hierarchy system. During a bus ride on an outing in the country, each senior high school student sat with a group of junior high school students. For a period of two hours, English knowledge was handed down from the older to the younger students in a way signifi-cantly different from any kind of memorized patterns. The younger learned from the older in a social milieu similar to the ancient Japanese school. The contract goal of foreign language learning was transformed through the social dynamics of the age hierarchy into a value operant in the ESS group.

9.4.2. Learning Atmosphere

After the Gasshuku, one student remarked that he was "Happy to be returning to Japan again" although he had not left Japan to begin with. However, the atmosphere of the Gasshuku was compared to a trip to the United States. Through the cultural mechanism of the Gasshuku, an experience with American culture provided motivation for each student to accept the CLL discipline for English speaking for a period of twenty-four hours. Violations of the English-speaking rule were punished as part of the interaction goals of the Gasshuku, as has been described. Through the cultural norms of the Gasshuku in the prohibition of Japanese and the enforcement of English speaking, interaction goals were transformed into interaction values.

9.4.3. Anxiety

A supportive learning atmosphere lessened the anxiety natural to Japanese speakers. After the Gasshuku, the older students remarked that, through the preparations for the Gasshuku, they had achieved significant social learning for life even as high school students. In having to deal with foreigners over the telephone in English, they had learned some important lessons in handling human relationships. In addition to foreign language mastery, the preparations filled the needs of the students for personal development. Consequently, the need goal became a need value in the negotiations for the contract. Additionally, all contract negotiations were carried out on the senior level in English.

9.4.4. Silence

The most significant finding of this experiment (conducted in 1971 and 1972) was the connection between silence and learning. Even silence can contribute to foreign-language learning. During the experiment when reflection did not function overtly, one of the most dramatic impressions of the ESS Gasshuku was the living cultural mechanism of silence through which foreign-language learning occurred as both a need and process value of the group. During the ESS-Gasshuku, the members were seated around a single table in busy preparation for English speeches. The group maintained silence for over an hour, a silence all the more striking because the students were at ease and working. Silence functioned as a process value to be sought after by all. Through kinesthetic communication, the rattling of papers, the sound of writing, an occasional cough, the shifting of body position, the members conveyed to each other the silent message that they were busy performing the group activity. The Gasshuku reinforced the discipline of CLL for foreign-language speaking but, in its own way, it imposed a mechanism of silence that greatly contributed to foreign-language learning. At the end of the silent period, each member produced a very lively and humorous speech in English.

Previously, the value of silence was operative in other CLL groups but in a different way. In addition to fewer periods of silence, a CLL group of Spanish speakers at the University of Michigan were irked by the silence and, before long, they were arguing with each other. Usually, these arguments occurred between two people. The other members of the group would listen in silence. At times, the listeners would make comments upon the humorous aspects of the situation. Conversation was stimulated, but the vehemence was also kept within the bounds of a learning situation.

Americans tended to grow very anxious when periods of silence occurred during CLL group sessions. The need for silence certainly was there, because periods of silence invariably occurred. During the silence, they began to repeat sentences from the lesson which others had previously spoken. In other words, to fill the periods of silence, the members of an American CLL group drilled themselves in the foreign language. They learned from the process value of silence operative in a CLL group, but in a manner different from the Japanese and the Spanish groups.

The Spanish, American, and Japanese groups learned foreign language, but in a different relationship to the process value of silence. The dynamic relationship between silence and foreign language learning was clarified in Chapter 6. The experiments at Nanzan showed the effectiveness of foreign-language learning in small group communities making full use of living domestic cultural mechanisms involving the whole personality and life space of the individual.

9.4.5. Summary

The task of this chapter was to describe, classify, and show how culture mechanisms work. Culture mechanisms were classified in Part 1, described in greater detail in Part 2, and exemplified in Part 3. The Japanese case with CLL demonstrates two important conclusions: first, given the right culture-learning mechanisms, the group process leads to social learning centered on values (Chapter 3) even in extracurricular groups; second, it demonstrates how language and culture interrelate in a specific learning environment. These conclusions are of importance not only to foreign-language teachers, but also to linguists, anthropologists, and others interested in human learning. Our common efforts to understand how people learn will further our knowledge of language and culture.

Chapter 10
Interviewing with Community Language Learning

10.0.

The purpose of this chapter is to introduce a series of interpersonal exercises as solutions to problems commonly encountered by teachers of English conversational skills. The whole series can be implemented or each exercise can be used independently. The approach need not be CLL. In the Japanese case with CLL, the "Interview" takes on interpersonal functions and characteristics which appear in Japanese society at large.

PART 1: INTERVIEWING WITH CLL

10.1.0.

In Part 1, some practical solutions to the problems sketched in earlier chapters are offered. I have used a series of structured interviews with junior college female students at Nanzan Junior College. The classes, required by the curriculum, met twice a week for ninety minutes per class. These interview exercises can be used with foreign languages other than English at intermediate and advanced levels of ability. Since each interview can also be used separately, they may be used as a change of pace when the students become bored with a textbook. With proper attention to group life, the combination of exercises can be put together by any teacher to provide for the personal development of the individual while English-speaking ability is being acquired.

An understanding of the interpersonal function of the Interview in Japanese society will further clarify what is meant by group life. The Interview is a highly flexible interpersonal phenomenon which is employed when a crisis arises during the life of a Japanese group. The public life of the group is interrupted for a time. A series of private meetings in pairs or small groups is held between the leaders and among the different factions of the same group. These meetings take on the interpersonal configuration of an informal interview. They are held in a flexible way in pairs, small groups, and in larger meetings of representatives from differing factions. The timing of these small meetings or interviews is considered very sensitive; otherwise the highly charged emotional atmosphere might lead to a permanent rupture of the group's unity. The purpose of the small meetings is to dispel unfounded rumors and suspicions, to promote mutual understanding, and to redefine the roles of all the leaders and participants. When the confidence of the members has risen to the point where a fresh and unanimous consensus is possible, the public life of the group is reconvened with ceremony and celebration.

During the Interview, a number of listening, observing, and questioning skills are employed in order to promote mutual understanding. These same skills, if applied within the group life of a foreign language class, can be a very powerful force for individual learning. With a proper understanding and use of the Interview as it functions in Japanese culture, the following five exercises greatly contribute to learning: "The Johari Window," "An Introduction to Creative Communication," "An Interview with You," "An Interview with the Teacher" and "A Personal Interview." An additional short reading entitled "The Distinction Between Content and Process" can be introduced at any time according to the teacher's discretion. The Interview enhances learning through the approximation and application of Japanese patterns of interaction at each CLL stage.

10.1.1. The Interview at Stage I

Stage I is the Birth Stage. Japanese students at this stage are hardly capable of producing any kind of English sentence. They have been trained to memorize lists of vocabulary and to translate from English into Japanese and *vice versa*. They have no experience in using English as a vehicle of interpersonal communication. Since Japanese do not normally communicate in English among themselves, the first task of the teacher is to establish the life of the group through communication among the students themselves. Japanese culture provides an interpersonal mechanism which can be of great assistance in establishing group life. The group contract can be initiated through self-introduction in small groups. Each person presents his self-history, general interests, and specific purpose for joining the group. A tape recorder inserted into the group will help keep the attention focused on English learning. The individual becomes identified as a member of the community through Self-introduction. The students' discovery of their identity as English speakers contributes greatly to the reduction of anxiety.

After self-introduction, the permissiveness connected with small group activities can be avoided by reconvening the whole group. The "Johari Window" is introduced by way of reflection on the small group self-introduction. An overhead projector can be used to present the explanation to the class. Some of the physical fatigue connected with language learning can also be alleviated with the use of audiovisual equipment, such as a tape recorder or overhead projector. The Johari Window serves to introduce the student to his "English-speaking Self" (cf. Curran, 1972, 130). "Johari" is an abbreviation of Joseph Luft (1963, 10–15) and Harry Ingram, who first described a "windowlike" model for communication based on self-understanding. There are four sections in the window: the Arena, the Blind Spot, the Facade, and the Mystery. The section open to the self and the other, the public area, is called "the Arena." The second section, closed to the self but open to the other, is called "the Blind Spot." The third part, open to the self but closed to the other, is called "the Facade." The fourth part is called "the Mystery" because it is closed to the self and the other. Each person possesses all four areas; each influences communication. The walls between each section of the window are permeable and change with each communication situation. Information moves across the boundaries from the Mystery to the Facade where a person can choose whether it will come into the Arena by sharing it with another. Information can also pass from the Mystery into the Blind Spot. When others reveal this information, the individual concerned may be shocked. Cultural shock may be treated in this connection. If the mystery of self is faced with courage, then communication relationships can be established with others in the Arena. Insights into the mystery of self can be gained through communicating with others. After the explanation, students can be asked to construct a Johari Window in relation to their small groups. Covert issues in the class which may be causing anxiety can then be discussed openly. The life of the group is firmly established on growth in self-understanding through communicating with others. The class itself becomes an arena for the open discussion and solution of all the problems which may arise in the course of the life of the group.

10.1.2. The Interview at Stage II

Stage II is the Childhood Stage. In this stage, the individual begins to express meanings and initiate exchanges with others. Two exercises together called "An Introduction to Creative Communication" serve to focus the direction and identity of the group upon the basic skills required for foreign language communication. These exercises also define a clear social structure in which students can practice communication with each other.

The first exercise is called "Rogerian Listening" (Simon et al., 1972; 1978, 295–8). The class is divided into triads. One person presents a topic, problem or theme. The second person must repeat both the content of the message and the feeling behind the words before giving a reaction or opinion. The third person is the time keeper and observer. The interaction is timed to last ten minutes. Then the roles are exchanged until each person has had a chance to perform all three roles.

Reflection on the exercise revealed some interesting points. First, the pace of the communication was slowed down considerably. Consequently, the individuals had time to consider the message before attempting a reply. The result was an improvement in the grammatical quality of the reaction. Students of intermediate ability had time to make grammatical adjustments in their English. Second, the exercise caused a great amount of physical fatigue. The students realized that listening is an active faculty that consumes much energy. At the same time, students of basic ability improved their performance as a result of increased listening concentration. Third, the experience of observing the interaction of two persons helped the observer to understand that the difficulty of mastering a foreign language is the struggle towards mutual understanding. In the highly-charged affective atmosphere, grammatical forms and meanings communicated in an exact way were less easily forgotten. Advanced students began to correct each others' grammar in a highly unobtrusive manner. When the observer was an advanced learner, knowledge of the foreign language was also communicated to a less advanced participant. Individual differences in ability were bridged· during the performance of Rogerian

Listening. Fourth, Rogerian Listening was not a completely satisfying experience because listening is only a single skill. The slow pace of the communication was unnatural and even frustrating. Other skills employed in communication include making statements, asking questions, and answering.

The second exercise is called "Asking, Answering and Observing." One person (A) presents a problem or topic of conversation. The next person (B) assists the first in developing the topic. The message is repeated briefly and then B is allowed to ask supportive questions in order to help A develop his theme. Supportive questions are introduced by "Who," "What," "Where," "When," "Why," and "How." Questions which can be answered with "Yes" or "No" do not help the individual, but serve merely to satisfy the curiosity of the listener. Supportive questions help develop the communication. The observer (C) keeps the time and takes notes on significant phases of the interaction. After ten minutes, the roles are interchanged so that each participant receives a chance to perform in all three roles: asking, answering and observing.

In order to avoid boredom, the reflection period was structured around a checklist. The performance of person B (the questioner) was evaluated by A (the person answering) and *vice versa*. The observer (C) evaluated the interaction between both A and B. The checklist for A contained the following questions about B's conduct: Could you speak freely? Were the questions easy to understand? Could you really reveal your thoughts? Checklist B about A's conduct contained the following questions: Were you anxious during the session? Did A really open up to your questions? Did you understand A's answers or attempt to clarify them? Checklist C, about the conduct of both A and B, contained the following questions: Were both A and B relaxed in the relationship? Were the questions and answers mutually supportive? Did mutual trust exist? What about the gestures, the tone of voice, and the mannerisms of both A and B? As a result of these two exercises, the understanding of self and the other, the meaning of the Johari Window, was greatly deepened. At the same time, the direction and identity of the group were firmly focused on the acquisition of the foreign language.

10.1.3. The Interview at Stage III

At Stage III, the Separate Existence Stage, the learner begins to function in an independent way in the foreign language. The strong urge to individual performance can be greatly enhanced by a pair-group exercise called "An Interview With You." This interview was patterned after an exercise from *Caring and Sharing in the Foreign Language Classroom* by Gertude Moskowitz (1978, 54–55). This interview is a guided conversation. A series of open-ended statements and questions are printed on a single page of a small booklet. Rogerian Listening is also reintroduced during the conversations. The participants are led through the program to explore mutual goals and values in learning. The individuals are allowed a certain amount of freedom in deciding their own progress through the program. The students were given the choice of performing the interview inside or outside the classroom. Permissiveness was avoided by asking the students to note down the percentage of foreign language they intended to use before the exercise began.

By way of reflection, the students were asked to compare the percentage of English they actually used with the percentage promised before the exercise. The non-judgemental way in which the teacher allowed the students to evaluate their own progress resulted in a strong wish to repeat the exercise with a different partner. When this occurred, I agreed on the condition that the students would prepare a set of questions or open-ended statements to be asked of the teacher. This condition set the stage for the re-entry of the teacher into the community. Small group exercises give the students the chance to use the basic English they have acquired. But contact with the teacher is also necessary if the students hope to progress to more advanced levels of ability.

10.1.4. The Interview at Stage IV

Stage IV is the Reversal Stage. In the first three CLL stages the teacher has functioned in a role of understanding the students. At Stage IV, the roles of the teacher and participants are redefined in order for advanced learning to occur through an exercise called "An Interview With the Teacher." At Stage IV the teacher adopts the role of interviewee or client. The whole class becomes the interviewer or counselor. The questions from the previous exercise are collected and put in order according to life history. The students are allowed to ask about the childhood, adolescence, and university life of the teacher. Repetitive questions are discarded and the students compose new ones where gaps exist. I gathered a series of fifty-two questions from the students. Employing all the skills which they had learned in creative communication, each student was allowed to ask two questions of the teacher. In order to enhance the experience, I brought pictures of my early life and student days for the students to examine.

10.1.5. The Interview at Stage V

Stage V is the Adult Stage. After a forty-five-minute interview with the teacher as interviewee, the roles were reversed again. The students were assigned the task of conducting interviews among themselves. The exercise, patterned after Hopper and Whitehead (1979, 223–352), was called "A Personal Interview." The first purpose of the interview was to provide a chance for the participants to develop English speaking fluency. The second purpose was to help the interviewee establish better self-understanding by a review of past life history and future goals. The exercise consisted of three parts: preparing, conducting, and evaluating the interview. By way of preparation, each group of five students composed a single set of open-ended statements and questions covering the life history of a student from childhood, through junior and senior high school, and into junior college. Future hopes and goals were also included. In conducting the ten-minute interview, one student acted as interviewer; one student became the interviewee; and the other two were the observers. The interview was followed by a brief evaluation session structured in the following way: the interviewee gave her opinion about the interview; the observers and the time keeper then gave their observations. After listening to all these opinions in silence, the interviewer was allowed to speak and explain her conduct. Following a brief interval of personal reflection, the roles were changed and the interview was repeated with the same set of questions.

Since the students also expressed confusion regarding the purpose of the interviews, a short reading called "The Distinction between Content and Process" was introduced to clarify the content and interpersonal aspects of the learning situation. This reading helped students to distinguish the task (learning to speak English fluently) from the process (the development of mutual self-understanding). The students began to understand the distinction when the exercise was repeated a second time, deviating from the previous set of questions if necessary. The effects of the interview were felt both inside and outside the classroom. Inside the classroom, the focus of the foreign language learning was on the personal welfare and development of each participant. Outside the school, students began to apply the distinction to job interviews which were crucial in determining future careers after graduation. They reported afterward that they were more relaxed during these job interviews.

PART 2: SUMMARY

10.2.0.

The result of using Interviews with CLL was "whole-person" learning. The individual was fully involved at each CLL stage. At Stage I, the Johari Window produced a sense of something valuable which extended beyond the scope of foreign-language learning into the daily life of the learner. Understanding of self and others was deepened during Stage II by the cultivation of listening, asking, answering and observing skills. Whole-person learning penetrated deeply into the consciousness of the individual. Therefore, it was an easy task for the learner to transfer and apply these skills to life outside the classroom. At Stage III, those skills were applied in a very intensive way in an interview with just one other person. This interview was instrumental in establishing English speaking relationships among the Japanese students themselves. One of the biggest needs in the English education field today is for the Japanese to establish communications relationships in English among themselves. There are signs that this is beginning to occur during meetings of English teachers when non-native speakers are present. However, the real need is to see English being used as a medium for the increase of mutual understanding not only between Japanese and foreigners, but also among Japanese themselves.

During the exercises for Stages II and III, the pauses for individual reflection served to relieve the physical fatigue connected with speaking a foreign language for a protracted period of time. At Stage IV, the students were strongly impressed by the conduct of the teacher. They realized that they were dealing with a fellow human being with a life history similar in some respects to their own. For a teacher to appear human is, apparently, an extraordinary phenomenon in Japanese education. Consequently, when the roles were reversed at Stage V, the teacher became a more powerful model for the conduct of the students. Without any suggestion or assignment, the students brought all their personal pictures on the day appointed for conducting the interviews. This happened in such a completely spontaneous way that class order was interrupted for a time. After an exchange of pictures, the students settled down and adopted their roles in a serious manner.

Students have different needs at all stages of development. There are no magical formulae for success in teaching a foreign language. The timing of the exercises is crucial to the progress of the group and the individual and a skillful monitoring of the atmosphere of the class is necessary at all times. The teacher has the ultimate responsibility for deciding the best way to use these exercises. I have selected and described a few in such a way that any teacher can rewrite and adapt them according to the needs of the students. It is the teacher's judgement which structures the learning context.

Chapter 11

Self-concept in Foreign Language Learning: Some Space Explorations

11.0. Introduction

The task of this chapter is to explore self-concept through what Andrews (1977, 43) has called "Self-fulfilling Prophecy." Self-concept is the touch-stone of personal orientation, and from the concept of self, each person generates a network of expectations, behaviors, and interpretations of events which are consistent with it. Self-concept works in a circular rather than in a linear way. Besides reaching out, each individual forms a personal environment, a psychological space. Through feedback from others or by personal reflection, we are confirmed in a given identity and sense of community, as will be shown in Part 1.

Space is connected with communication inside the self and with others. Even the space configurations of our classrooms (physical space) are based on implicit definitions and agreements. If these implicit contracts are explored, clarified or challenged, how would learning progress be affected? The purpose of Part 2 is to explore and introduce questions that can be answered by further research. The substitution of a circle for the linear—rectangular space configuration of our classrooms may bring about a signifi-cant change in communication patterns. Besides psychological and physical space, social, cultural, and learner space can also influence learning progress. These dimensions of space will be touched upon with reference to further research in the future.

PART 1: PSYCHOLOGICAL SPACE —
A SELF-FULFILLING PROPHECY

11.1.0. Psychological Space

The purpose of Part 1 is to introduce the concept of psychological space as a "Self-fulfilling Prophecy" (Andrews, 1977). Self-concept is formed in a circular way through confirmation from others and by selectively shunting aside actions and experiences incongruent with the image of the self. We establish a negative feedback loop that keeps change at a manageable level. By so doing, we form a psychological space that confirms us in a given identity and sense of continuity. But growth is also a basic human appetite. We seek not only continuity, but also novelty. Within limits, we are willing to risk moving out from familiar space configurations in exchange for the possibility of wider exploration. Given some confidence in our ultimate ability to cope, we will from time to time initiate experiences that are different from the way we see ourselves, and by so doing, make the spatial world hang together a bit differently.

11.1.1. Self-fulfilling Prophecy

Both sides of self-concept, the part that confirms our identity and the part that invites novelty and change, explain many of our successes and failures in foreign-language education. The excuses Japanese make for their inability to speak English and other foreign languages provides a good example of the negative feedback loop. Personal and interpersonal processes, according to Andrews (1977, 43), interact to form a self-fulfilling prophecy consisting of seven phases. Process A, which will be called "Can't Speak," is made up of perceived feelings, attitudes, physical capacities, and so on – who we are and who we are not. Out of this core, we generate feelings, needs, and attitudes toward specific people and situations, for instance, toward native speakers of English. If a Japanese considers himself a poor speaker of English, a great amount of anxiety will be generated in the face of an English-speaking situation. Because self-concept is linked to expectations and feelings toward others, Process B in the case of Japanese speakers of English can be termed "Anxiety." These feelings and expectations flow into action (Process C). This does not mean that all feeling automatically develops into action, but rather that behavior has a recognizable relation to the self-image of the one who initiates it. Thus we see Process C, for convenience "Doesn't Speak," appearing in Japanese groups when the responsibility is shunted to one or two individuals who are deemed more capable. They are forced into the extremely uncomfortable role of English-speaking "representative" for the whole group.

We tend to act in ways that will get us treated as the persons we believe we are. This meets the needs of the initiator and is also a message to others, a set of cues from which they form an image (Process D) of the person with whom they are dealing. This image, while rarely an exact duplicate of the person's own self-picture, will significantly overlap it. This is because, as each process shades into the next, the person selects (often unconsciously) attitudes and behavior congruent with his self-concept and rejects those which do not fit. A prevalent image among Japanese is that they can't speak English, but the image among non-Japanese is that Japanese won't speak foreign languages. Therefore, Process D will be called "Won't Speak." The result is that we "train" people to see us and respond in ways to which we are accustomed. Of course, this match is not perfect; the other in turn will have his filters, so that how the other reacts is far more than a mirror of our own expectations, but the tendency is there. This is represented by the others' impressions (Process D) and others' actions (Process E). Thus we find Japanese entering specialized schools for foreign language with split personalities; they receive treatment in accord with their self-concept as English speakers. They find themselves in classes of advanced level in grammar, reading, and writing, but at basic levels in speaking ability. For convenience, Process E will be termed "Can't–Doesn't–Won't Speak." The negative affect is strongest at this point.

Whenever the actions of others (Process E) are in accord with our self-concept, it is relatively easy to understand and assimilate communications from them. However, when others present us with novelty and surprise, this may produce anxiety. If so, we have resources to eliminate any undesirable dissonance. By selective perception (Process F), we simply block out or minimize cues that are discordant with how we want to be treated. In the Japanese case with English, Process F is referred to as "Can't–Doesn't Speak." As a native speaker of English, I have often been confronted with the anomaly of Japanese speakers vehemently claiming in grammatically perfect and appropriate English, as well as at great length, what poor speakers of foreign language they really were. No amount of encouragement or persuasion could convince such speakers that they were really adept at foreign language. When we are unable to avoid perceiving such cues from the environment, it is still possible to interpret, redefine, or deny responsibility for them in some way (Process G). This minimizes the other's disruptive impact on our self-concept. In the Japanese case at Process G, the "Doesn't Speak" is reinterpreted and transformed into a stronger "Can't Speak." Thus we maintain a complete negative feedback cycle, beginning and ending with the certainties of self. We define much of our experience of the world in the process. This includes the speaking of English and other foreign languages in the Japanese case.

11.1.2. Reflection

Intrapsychically, we often engage in the same process by responding to our own actions via selective perception and interpretation, thereby maintaining an internal stability cycle (that is, we move from Process C to Process F). This is a self-reflexive inner version of the full cycle, with an internalized image playing the part of the other. In short, the process outlined above constitutes a self-fulfilling prophecy, anchored in the expectations stemming from one's self-concept. It is also operative at every step in Japanese speakers of English and other foreign languages. This self-fulfilling prophecy is made up of a vicious circle which is difficult to break because of its strong affective component.

PART 2: SOME SPATIAL EXPLORATIONS

11.2.0. Integrating Principles

The psychological space attending self-concept was outlined in Part 1. Self-concept reveals itself in strong affects which are difficult to deal with. Perhaps by changing the spatial configurations of our classrooms, some understanding and change will be brought about in the effectiveness of our teaching. Andrews (1977, 44) has suggested four integrating principles that are related to space. First, it is important to follow the learner's leads; certain places in the cycle will be most salient and ready for work at any given moment. The spatial make-up of our classrooms in rows of desks with a podium at the front dictates one kind of communication from the teacher to the students. It is possible to substitute other space configurations (in spite of the fact that, in most Japanese universities, the desks are riveted to the floor). The revision of space prepares the student for a different kind of communication from the teacher, as will be shown later. A second principle to keep in mind is that all seven processes are linked and that the overall goal is increased speaking ability. Physical space is linked to social space. Reciprocal actions involving others occur in social space (Processes C, D, and E). Some students find their usual learning world smashed and torn to pieces by the spatial configurations of CLL. This is especially true in the case of Japanese learners who are extremely sensitive to changes in space. For effective learning to occur, the world must be put back together and restored to integrity. Respect for the social space of the student must be encouraged by the teacher at all times. Since one is attempting to improve the overall flow from self-concept through interaction and interpretation of events and back again to self-concept, the teacher should deal with blockages in that flow. Speakers are usually most aware of their anxiety, therefore it may prove to be effective to begin with Process B. Lastly, both awareness and change are necessary, but *not necessarily in that order.* When the student has become self-aware, he should be encouraged to use that awareness to initiate change and, when the student finds himself at the peak of new progress, it is helpful to stimulate understanding so that the student has a clear picture of where he stands.

11.2.1. Process B: Anxiety

Spatial changes give a tone to a communication, accent it, and at times even override the spoken word (Hall, 1973, 180). The flow and shift of distance between people as they interact with each other is part and parcel of the communication process. Our classrooms dictate the kind of communication which occurs even before the teacher and the student enter the rooms. The deck is stacked before the lesson begins. This can be seen if we compare the linear—rectangular space configuration of our classrooms with that of CLL groups. The traditional classroom is square or rectangular with desks arranged in straight rows. Allowing for variations, the podium is placed in front and, in very traditional settings, is even elevated. The communication is unidirectional from the teacher to the students. In contrast, the CLL configuration is circular. The physical design of the Type I experience dictates one form of communication. The teacher participates but does not force the activity. The spatial form of a Type II experience presupposes a different type of communication and role for the teacher. The small groups are another variation of the circular configuration with the teacher placed outside the groups. The teacher does not participate but stands ready to assist during a Type II experience. The multiplication of small circles fosters communication among the students and allows the teacher to move from group to group when help is needed. The Type III experience occurs in a different spatial form. The students are arranged in pairs forming two lines. In this form, the students can move in an orderly way from place to place very quickly. Brief communication with many individuals is allowed. The role of the teacher is ambiguous because the teacher's participation is optional. The space configuration of the Type III experience allows for flexibility in determining the teacher's role. As opposed to a linear—rectangular form, the basic spatial configuration of the CLL class is the circle that can be used in a flexible way to promote communication.

11.2.2. Process C: Doesn't Speak: Social Space

In American culture, we interpret space between people in terms of four zones surrounding each person: the intimate zone, the personal zone, the businesslike zone, and the public zone (Hopper and Whitehead, 1979, 112–13). In America, a person who stands less than two feet away from one would, in most instances, have to be a close friend or family member. This is the intimate zone. At a distance of two to four feet, the personal zone, Americans tend to be comfortable only if they are fairly well acquainted with the other person. The businesslike zone (five to eight feet) is the distance at which Americans usually stand when they meet for the first time. The inner edge of the businesslike zone is the distance you stand from another during a very formal business handshake (Hopper and Whitehead, 1979, 113).

How do these zones affect progress in second language learning? The traditional classroom, seemingly, is designed to keep people apart in either the public or businesslike zones. How can we expect students to make progress in speaking ability if we keep them apart? If students have never had the opportunity of a foreign-language speaking experience at intimate or personal distance, how can we expect them to function comfortably in the businesslike or public zones? The CLL Type II and III experiences allow communication at closer distances. The businesslike and public zones are accounted for by the Type I experience. More flexibility in utilizing all four zones is necessary if we hope to give students a chance to change from the "Doesn't Speak" position to a more positive appreciation of foreign-language speaking.

11.2.3. Process D: Won't Speak: Territoriality

Process D is the image which Japanese project as non-speakers even though many possess the ability to speak a foreign language. The image is connected with the concept of territoriality. Territoriality is usually defined as behavior by which an organism characteristically lays claim to an area and defends it against members of its own species (Hall, 1969, 7). The following incident illustrates how this concept affects progress in speaking a foreign language. In the spring of 1981, I was having a particularly difficult time with students who were extremely anxious during a Type I experience. All the previous solutions didn't seem to work. I substituted Type II and III experiences and returned to the Type I experience only after several lessons from a textbook. Nothing seemed to work; the students remained passive and silent. Then they suggested that I appoint a discussion leader. In previous CLL activity, more effective results occurred when the students were given responsibility in pairs. So rather than a single student, two students were appointed to act as moderators of the discussion during a Type I experience. That broke the ice and the group responded with active participation. The students were much more at ease. Obviously, the covert message given to the group was: take the responsibility. The reply was a request for territory in which to operate. Once the territory was given, the speaking activity grew more lively. The discussion leader role was rotated so that each student had a chance to assume responsibility for the group conversation. The sharing of responsibility brought about a significant rise in the degree of participation. This is but a single illustrative example of how the concept of territoriality can affect progress in speaking ability.

11.2.4. Process E: Can't–Won't–Doesn't Speak: Extensions

Process E consists of the actions of others toward Japanese who can't speak English. Ultimately, the speaker creates his own world; and therefore, in order to help Japanese learners, we have to look at spatial extensions of territoriality (Hall, 1973, 102). The territory is in every sense of the word an extension of the organism. Man has created material extensions of territoriality as well as visible and invisible markers. Fixed feature space, semi-fixed space and informal space are degrees of territoriality. Fixed feature space is one of the basic ways of organizing the activities of individuals and groups. It includes material manifestations as well as the hidden, internalized designs that govern behavior. The important point about fixed feature space is that it is the mold in which a great deal of behavior is cast. During the course of this book, many suggestions for a fresh approach to learning have taken into account the basic structure of our classroom activity, but more has to be done to bring about effective ways of dealing with learning problems. A semi-fixed space design such as the circular configuration of CLL contributes to congruence between design and function. A variety of spaces give people a chance to be involved or not, as the occasion and mood of the class demands. The proper structuring of semi-fixed features can have a profound effect on behavior. This effect is measurable (Hall, 1973, 110).

Informal space consists of distance outside our awareness. Hall (1973, 112) has called this category informal space because it is unstated, not because it lacks form or has no importance. Informal space patterns have distinct bounds and such deep, if unvoiced, significance that they form an essential part of culture. These bounds influence progress in foreign language and can contribute to learning if they are clarified through reflection.

11.2.5. Process F: Can't–Doesn't Speak: Context

One of the functions of culture is to provide a highly selective screen between man and the outside world. In its many forms, therefore, culture designates what we pay attention to and what we ignore (Hall, 1976, 85). The screening function provides structure for the world and protects the nervous system from an overload of information. One way to handle the overload is to program the memory of the system so that less information is required for activating it. The programming is done in the social context rather than in the language used. In a high context culture, the context carries most of the information and meaning. Without context, the meaning of the message is difficult to understand. The code is incomplete since it encompasses only part of the message. More attention to the context in which we teach and learn should help us to understand the nature of selective perception and its effects on learning progress in the future. In low context cultures, the words carry more weight than the social context. Besides memorizing sentences, learners have to cope with context, especially between American and Japanese cultures where the contrasts between high and low context are so strong. Japanese learners have to appreciate and pay attention to the meaning and expression of language; Americans, especially teachers, have to become more sensitive to the context in which meanings are exchanged.

11.2.6. Process G: Can't Speak: Culture Space

Given the open situation of CLL, Japanese learners define the space according to their culture norms. Foreign language learning gives Japanese a chance to learn different norms and to understand their own. One of their unspoken norms is that they do not speak foreign language with other Japanese. This norm is slowly changing as can be seen from the activity of a CLL Type II experience. Once Japanese can be convinced to speak among themselves, even more significant changes and improvements will come about. This is a task for the future.

11.2.7. Process A: Can't Speak

The change in self-image from non-speaker to speaker occurs in learner space. Learner space is the key for an understanding of psychological, physical, social and cultural space. These are forms of the space given by the teacher to the learner. At the beginning of this chapter self-concept was explained through a self-fulfilling prophecy. Both sides of self-concept, the part that insures continuity and the part that induces change, are connected with space exploration. I would like to conclude this book with an appeal for trust in the learner. We have to nourish both sides of self-concept if we hope to see results in the classroom. We have to propose the limits of a psychological contract in order to insure that the learner, in his prophetic self, is able to see the necessary changes that have to occur in acquiring a new language. We have to trust the learner and allow innovations which represent an advance in learning. Perhaps future research will conclude that learner-space is the greatest gift that the teacher can give to the learner. In return, the learner's gift to the teacher may be an increased sensitivity and understanding of how people learn a foreign language.

Bibliography

Andrews, J. Personal change and intervention style. *Journal of Humanistic Psychology,* 1977, 17, 41–63.

Argyle, M. *Bodily Communication.* London: Methuen & Co., 1975.

Barnlund, D. *Public and Private Self in Japan and the United States: Communicative Style of Two Cultures.* Tokyo: The Simul Press, 1975.

Begin, Y. *Evaluative and Emotional Factors in Learning a Foreign Language.* Paris: Desclee & Cie (Bellarmin), 1971.

Berwick, R. Staging classroom discussion. *TESOL Quarterly,* 1975, 9, 282–8.

Birdwhistell, R. *Kinesics and Context: Essays on Bodily Motion Communication.* Philadelphia: University of Pennsylvania Press, 1970.

Bixenstine, E. The value-fact antithesis in behavioral science. *Journal of Humanistic Psychology,* 1976, 16 (2), 35–37.

Bradford, L. Developing potentialities through class groups. In C. G. Kemp (Ed.), *Perspectives on the Group Process.* Boston: Houghton Mifflin, 1970.

Brooks, N. Teaching culture in the foreign language classroom. In *The Florida F. L. Reporter,* 1969, 7 (1), (Special Anthology Issue), 20–28.

Brown, H. D. Affective variables in second language acquisition. *Language Learning,* 1973, 23, 231–44.

The English teacher as researcher. *English Language Teaching Journal,* 1977, 31, 274–9.

Bugental, J. *The Search for Authenticity: An Existential-Analytic Approach to Psychotherapy.* New York: Holt, Rinehart & Winston, 1965.

Butler, J. The iconic mode in psychotherapy. In D. A. Wexler and L. Rice (Eds.), *Innovations in Client-Centered Therapy.* New York: John Wiley & Sons, 1974, 171–203.

Byrne, D. *Teaching Oral English.* London: Longman Group, 1976.

Chomsky, N. *Language and Mind.* (Enlarged edition). New York: Harcourt, Brace, Jovanovich, 1972.

Clark, M. Second language acquisition as a clash of consciousness. *Language Learning,* 1976, 26, 277–390.

Condon, J. and Yousef, F. *An Introduction to Intercultural Communication.* Indianapolis: Bobbs Merrill, 1975.

Corbluth, J. Remediation or development? Some thoughts for English language teachers. *English Language Teaching Journal,* 1974, 28, 118–25.

Corder, P. *Introducing Applied Linguistics.* Harmondsworth, Middlesex, England: Penguin Education, 1973.

Coward, R., and Ellis, J. *Language and Materialism: Developments in Semiology and the Theory of Subject.* London: Routledge & Kegan Paul, 1977.

Crystal, D., and Davy, D. Stylistic analysis. In J. Allen and P. Corder (Eds.), *The Edinburgh Course for Applied Linguistics. Vol. 1, Readings for Applied Linguistics.* London: Oxford University Press, 1973. (Originally published 1969).

135

Crystal, D. Paralinguistics. In *The Body as a Medium of Expression*. J. Benthall and T. Polhemus (Eds.), New York: E. P. Dutton, 1975.

Curran, Charles. *Counseling and Psychotherapy: the Pursuit of Values*. New York: Sheed & Ward, 1968.

Religious Values in Counseling and Psychotherapy. New York: Sheed & Ward, 1969.

Counseling–Learning: A Whole Person Model for Education. New York: Grune & Stratton, 1972.

Counseling–Learning in Second Languages. Apple River, Illinois: Apple River Press, 1976.

A linguistic model for learning and living in the new age of the person. In C. Blatchford and J. Schachter (Eds.), *On TESOL '78: EFL Policies, Programs, Practices*. Washington, D.C.: TESOL, 1978(a).

Understanding: A Necessary Ingredient in Human Belonging. Apple River, Illinois: Apple River Press, 1978(b).

Dakin, J. *The Language Laboratory and Language Learning*. London: Longman Publishing Co., 1973.

Davis, L., and Keitges, D. Communication and values in the classroom. *Cross Currents*, 1979, 6, 33–62.

Dore, R. *Education in Tokogawa Japan*. London: Routledge & Kegan Paul, 1965.

Egan, G. *Encounter: Group Processes for Interpersonal Growth*. Belmont, CA: Brooks/Cole (Wadsworth Publishing Co.), 1970.

Elliot, A. V. The end of an epoch. *English Language Teaching Journal*, 1972, 26, 216–24.

Erikson, E. Identity and the life cycle. *Psychological Issues*, 1959, 1 (Whole No. 1).

Esper, E. A. *Mentalism and Objectivism in Linguistics*. New York: American Elsevier Publishing Co., 1968.

Ethical Principles in the Conduct of Research with Human Participants. Washington, D.C.: American Psychological Association, 1973.

Hall, E. *The Hidden Dimension*. New York: Anchor Press/Doubleday, 1969.

The Silent Language. New York: Doubleday, 1973.

Beyond Culture. Garden City, New York: Anchor Books/Doubleday, 1976.

Halliday, M. *Learning How to Mean: Explorations in the Development of Language*. London: Edward Arnold, 1975.

Harasawa, M. A critical survey of English language teaching in Japan. *ELTJ*, 1974, 29, 71–79.

Hawley, R., and Hawley, I. *Human Values in the Classroom*. New York: Hart Pub. Co., 1975.

Hirschmeier, J., and Yui, Y. *The Development of Japanese Business, 1600–1973*. (2nd edition). Cambridge, Mass.: Harvard University Press, 1981.

Hiyakawa, S. *Language in Thought and Action*, (3rd edition). New York: Harcourt, Brace, Jovanovich, 1972.

Hopper, J., and Whitehead, J. *Communication Concepts and Skills*. New York: Harper & Row, 1979.

Hughes, D. The silent period in group process. In C. G. Kemp (Ed.), *Prospectives on the Group Process: A Foundation for Counseling with Groups* (2nd edition). Boston: Houghton Mifflin Co., 1970.

Joos, M. *The Five Clocks*. New York: Harcourt, Brace & World, Inc., 1967.

Kanter, R. *Commitment Community: Communes and Utopias in Sociological Perspective*. Cambridge, Mass.: Harvard University Press, 1972.

Kluckhohn, F. Dominant and variant value orientation. In C. Kluckhohn, H. Murray, and D. Schneider (Eds.), *Personality In Nature, Society, and Culture* (2nd edition). New York: Alfred A. Knopf, 1971.

Kunihiro, M. An elephant in an antique shop. *Nucleus*, 1974, 27, 13–28(a).

Indigenous barriers to communication. *The Wheel Extended*, 1974, 3, 11–17(b).

Japanese language and intercultural communication. *The Japan Interpreter*, 1976, 10, 267–83.

Larsen-Freeman, D. A rationale for discourse analysis in second language acquisition research. In H. Brown, C. Yorio, and R. Crymes (Eds.), *On TESOL '78, Teaching and Learning English as a Second Language: Trends in Research and Practice*. Washington, D.C.: TESOL, 1977.

Lindsay, P. Language labs: Some reflections after ten years. *ELTJ*, 1973, 28, 5–10.

Luft, J. *Group Processes: An Introduction to Group Dynamics*. Palo Alto, California: The National Press, 1963.

Maslow, A. *The Psychology of Science: A Reconnaissance*. New York: Harper & Row, 1966.

Moskowitz, G. *Caring and Sharing in the Foreign Language Class*. Rowley, Mass.: Newbury House, 1978.

Nakane, C. *Japanese Society*. Berkeley and Los Angeles: University of California Press, 1970.

Peng, F. (Ed.) *Language in Japanese Society: Current Issues in Sociolinguistics*. Tokyo: The University of Tokyo Press, 1975.

Polanyi, M. *Scientific thought and social reality: essays by Michael Polanyi. Psychological Issues*, 1974, 8, (4, whole 32).

Pratt, S., and Tooley, J. Human actualization teams: the perspective of contract psychology. *American Journal of Orthopsychiatry*, 1966, 36, 881–95.

Raths, L., Harmin, M., and Simon, S. *Values and Teaching*. Columbus, Ohio: Charles E. Merrill, 1966.

Richards, J. Error analysis and second language acquisition. In J. Schumann and N. Stenson (Eds.), *New Frontiers in Second Language Learning*. Rowley, Mass.: Newbury House, 1974, 32–53.

Second Language Learning. In R. Wardhaugh and H. D. Brown (Eds.), *A Survey of Applied Linguistics*. Ann Arbor: The University of Michigan Press, 1976.

Roozeboom, W. The fallacy of the null-hypothesis significance test. In P. Badia, A. Haber and R. Runyon (Eds.), *Research Problems in Psychology*. Reading, Mass.: Addison-Wesley, 1970.

Saporta, S. Scientific grammars and pedagogical grammars. In J. B. Allen and P. Corder (Eds.), *The Edinburgh Course for Applied Linguistics, Vol. I, Readings for Applied Linguistics*. London: Oxford University Press, 1973. (Originally published in 1966).

Selinker, L. Interlanguage. In J. Schumann and N. Stenson (Eds.), *New Frontiers in Second Language Learning*. Rowley, Mass.: Newbury House, 1974, 114–36.

Sheflen, A. *How Behavior Means*. New York: Anchor Press, 1974.

Silva, C. Recent theories of language acquisition in relation to a semantic approach in foreign language teaching. *ELTJ*, 1975, 29, 337–46.

Simon, S., Howe, L., and Kirschenbaum, H. *Values Clarification: A Practical Handbook of Strategies for Teachers and Students*. New York: Hart Publishing Co., 1972/1978.

Stevick, E. The meaning of drills and exercises. *Language Learning*, 1974, 24, 1–22.

Teaching English as an alien language. In J. Fanselow and R. Crymes (Eds.),

On TESOL '76. Washington, D.C.: TESOL, 1976(a).

Memory, Meaning and Method: Some Psychological Perspectives on Language Learning. Rowley, Mass.: Newbury House, 1976(b).

Summary statement on counseling–learning and community language learning. *The Journal of Suggestive-Accelerative Learning and Teaching,* 1977, 2, 17–19.

Teaching Languages: A Way and Ways. Rowley, Mass.: Newbury House, 1980.

Vigil, N., and Oller, J. Rule fossilization: a tentative model. *Language Learning,* 1976, **26**, 281–95.

Von Eckartsberg, R. On experimental methodology. In F. Severin (Ed.), *Discovering Man in Psychology: A Humanistic Approach.* New York: McGraw Hill, 1973.

Wexler, D. A cognitive theory of experiencing, self-actualizing, and therapeutic process. In D. Wexler and L. Rice (Eds.), *Innovations in Client-Centered Therapy.* New York: John Wiley & Sons, 1974.

Wolf, R., and Tymitz, B. Ethnography and reading: matching inquiry mode to process. *Reading Research Quarterly,* 1976/1977, **12** (1), Guest Editorial.

Author Index

139

Subject Index

141